THE THREE CHIMNEYS

RECIPES & REFLECTIONS FROM THE
ISLE OF SKYE'S WORLD FAMOUS RESTAURANT

Shirley Spear

PHOTOGRAPHS BY ALAN DONALDSON

14117345

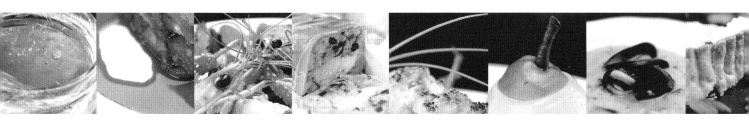

To Mum – you would have loved this.

First published in 2002 by Reekie Lums Enterprises
The Three Chimneys, Colbost, Dunvegan, Isle of Skye IV55 8ZT
in association with

Mercat Press
10 Coates Crescent, Edinburgh EH3 7AL

A CIP catalogue record for this book is available
from the British Library

ISBN 1 84183 043 7

Design and Art Direction: Peter McDermott
Printed by Butler & Tanner Ltd, Frome and London

At long last...

I KNEW IT!

After all the years I have been threatening to write 'The Book', I find myself up against the final, final deadline and still typing. Perhaps I do my best work under pressure, but I am notorious for rushing to pull everything together at the last possible moment. This includes finalising menus, much to the frustration of my chefs and waiting staff.

I always planned to devote a few quiet winter months to putting these pages together. Instead, I have been snatching odd hours between lunch and dinner service, working late, rising early. As I write, we are in the middle of July. Business is hectic. None of the publicity that has been showered upon us this year was planned or expected. How could we have imagined The Three Chimneys coming under such a huge spotlight as being included amongst the World's Top 50 restaurants?

Life has been a permanent race against time for me as a chef. Clock-watching and opening deadlines have contributed to the everyday stress of my kitchen. There is never enough oven time in the day to get everything baked to perfection, just as there is never enough preparation time to have every ingredient in a perfect state of

readiness before service begins. Chefs' nerves are stretched to the limit. But they thrive on it. Fired with adrenaline, the rush takes a hold. When orders are on, cooking becomes a precision juggling act. Slick timing is crucial. Nothing can be slapdash. 'Speed With Accuracy' are the watchwords.

Upon arriving at Colbost in the Isle of Skye, the idyllic setting of The Three Chimneys, on the sleepy shores of Loch Dunvegan, may seem a world apart from the reality of a busy kitchen in full swing. But the working lives we lead here are very full and highly intensive. Eddie and I have always had clear-cut roles within our business. He is in charge front-of-house and I am in the kitchen. Both jobs are fraught with sudden

three chimneys restaurant

changing circumstances, staff problems, delivery problems, customer demands and financial concerns that of course, the public never knows about. No two days are ever the same, but when the doors are open and the candles are lit, the stage is set and the play begins. The swing door between the kitchen and the dining rooms is like the theatre curtain. Every night is another critical performance.

We have always worked long hours and at times, I must admit that we show an unhealthy disregard for our own personal lives. After eighteen years we still live in the tiny flat above the restaurant, which means we are always on call. Days off and holidays have been too few and far between. The Three Chimneys has become our whole way of life.

We could never claim that our life in Skye has been a bed of roses, neither would we deny we have been forced from time to time into a love-hate relationship with island ways. Our success as a restaurant is partly due to our location and we will never underestimate the importance of the role Skye and its outstanding local produce has played in our success story.

For years, customers have been pressing me to write down the story of why we chose to run a restaurant in a remote corner of the Scottish Highlands. Their most frequently asked question is: "Why here?"

We were gloriously naïve when we bought The Three Chimneys, and if we knew then what we know now, we might never have gone through with the deal. Not only did we change our whole lifestyle, we moved from a busy main road near the centre of Croydon to a cottage by the sea down a single-track road with passing places. We also uprooted our young children; Steven who was aged five at the time, and Lindsay who was only just three. Our eighteen-year-old daughter, Sarah, was not ready to swap her city life for the wilds of Skye at that time and decided to stay in Croydon.

On reflection, it was an enormous step to take, but it was also typical of the spirit of our generation, many of whom moved into the countryside to start new lives. A number of our friends made similar decisions to change their lifestyle completely, but they had much safer qualifications to offer for work in other areas of the country, being teachers, broadcasters, artists and journalists.

We had no professional training or practical experience in the hospitality and catering industry. I had a yen to run a restaurant based upon my instinctive ability to cook, but nothing more. I was resolute that our restaurant's reputation would be based upon our unashamed promotion of all that was good about fresh Scottish food and the country's culinary heritage. We both wanted to create the kind of restaurant we ourselves would

hope to find if we were on holiday in Scotland. These were romantic ideals, rather than practical business plans, but the business would have been the poorer without them.

There can be no doubt that we struggled against many odds, money being the root of some of our crises. Local planning issues and a degree of island culture-shock were responsible for others. Despite the setbacks, our strength as a business has grown, much of

it gained from our intrinsic understanding of our customers' wishes and expectations, plus a natural enjoyment of our work.

For years, we knew that the only way the business would become more viable was to build accommodation and market The Three Chimneys all year round. There was a niche for five-star accommodation in north-west Skye and we knew that The Three Chimneys already attracted the right clientele to fill it. Again,

we were acting upon our instincts rather than formal market research. Our Bankers, however, could not be swayed. They could not agree that we would be capable of achieving the occupancy figures needed to sustain the borrowings we required to build six luxury bedroom suites, in a new building we were to call The House Over-By. The Bank was of the opinion that unless we offered full leisure facilities we would never achieve five-star status and

attract the right customers. They also had no confidence that we would be able to attract sufficient business over the winter months. We had to seek an alternative source of funding.

We opened The House Over-By in May 1999 and, thankfully, we have proved everybody wrong. Our new bedrooms have been immensely popular with our guests and have attracted an unprecedented amount of interest from the media. With the professional help and expertise of a local architect, builder, interior designer and marketing consultant, we had dared to be different. We had created accommodation with a "wow!" factor, previously unseen in the Highlands, with an exciting new brochure and graphics to match. Eddie and I were amazed at the level of goodwill towards the success of our project.

At the same time, we expanded the restaurant to occupy the whole of the ground floor of The Three Chimneys to include a small bar area. This involved major building work, knocking down the original staircase to our private flat that ran straight up through the middle of the house.

Our whole life mushroomed on an unexpected scale in rapid time. Having created several entirely new jobs, we suddenly found ourselves managing full-time, salaried staff. This was not an easy transition for either of us, particularly as we had to learn

to share major responsibilities with others. These ranged from taking a straightforward dinner reservation to handling our wages and accounts through our new computer. We came through it, older and more grey-haired, but a lot wiser for the whole experience.

Of all these new jobs, the most significant was the appointment of a sous chef. As I now had a strange and different role in so many wide ranging aspects of our business, it was essential to have someone skilled and reliable in the kitchen to act as my right hand. Isabel Tomlin joined us in April 1999. More superchef than sous chef, she is talented, versatile and works incredibly hard for The Three Chimneys. Writing this book would have been impossible without Issy's unrelenting support and encouragement. Never one to steal the limelight, I have managed to squeeze her into a few photographs, knowing she is quietly proud to have played such an important part in our more recent success stories.

The constant stream of media interest we attracted when we relaunched The Three Chimneys was baffling considering we had attracted so little, comparatively, in the past. One evening, I was in the kitchen about to launch into another busy service when I received a telephone call from Cate Devine. Cate was the editor of Scotland's *Saturday Herald Magazine* at this time. Her call came completely out of the blue. She was inviting me to contribute a regular monthly column to the magazine, with an article about a particular food ingredient together with relevant recipes. She would arrange to send a photographer to Skye to photograph the dishes at a mutually agreed time. The photographer turned out to be Alan Donaldson.

Having always dreamed, as a teenager, of being a journalist with my own column in a newspaper, the offer was one I could not refuse. The opportunity may have arrived thirty years late, but it was not one I was going to turn down readily. Most of the articles were written late at night and photographed on Sunday mornings. This was difficult, but I always made my deadlines.

This book is, in part, a collection of those articles as they first appeared in the *Saturday Herald* in the year 2000/01. I have adapted them slightly and have used many previously unpublished photographs taken at the time. Each chapter takes the reader through the calendar year, with some favourite recipes from the restaurant's kitchen. In addition, I have included my personal anecdotes relevant to the main subject of each chapter and its special time of the year. Collectively, these portray the background story of The Three Chimneys, some of my Scottish childhood memories and many other things that have influenced my style of cooking. I have also included some beautiful photographs of Skye landscapes, some scenes from the restaurant and snaps from our family albums.

This is not a full-blown cookery book, nor is it a detailed story of our life running one of Scotland's most popular restaurants. Treat it as a taste of more to follow and enjoy some of the flavour of my special restaurant in Skye. Here is The Three Chimneys.

In respect of the mighty oat

DID YOU know that in true respect of the mighty oat, a bowl of porridge should be eaten whilst standing up and walking around the room, from a birchwood bowl with a horn spoon? Porridge should always be made with a pinch of salt, and cream should be handed round in a separate bowl. The traditions connected with Scotland's national dish know no limits and stories of the Scot and his love of oats abound throughout history. There are umpteen references to oatmeal in the literature, poetry and song of centuries past. No matter where the ubiquitous Scot placed his feet upon dry land, it seems his oats went with him.

I am not a porridge fanatic, although I agree it is soothing, nourishing and warming on cold winter mornings. But I love using oatmeal in cooking. As a comfort food, the delicious, nutty aroma of oatmeal toasting in the oven is unique. I use the cooled and crunchy grains in a variety of sweet and savoury ways. There is no substitute. The intense, authentic flavour is a real treat when used with other ingredients. Its Scottish simplicity symbolises much of what I value in cooking.

At The Three Chimneys, I like to relate my menus to the simpler, basic ingredients of our culinary heritage. This seems to me to be particularly relevant because of our location. When travellers find their way here from all the far-flung corners of the globe, I believe it is important to relate the

food we serve to its very strong Scottish roots. Scotland's climate is highly suited to growing the best oat crop in the world. Oatmeal is said to be responsible for the brains and brawn of Scotland. This flower of Scottish soil is a healthy, nutritious food and it formed a staple part of the nation's daily diet for many generations.

Oatmeal and potatoes were ever-present in the life of a Highland crofter. Not so very long ago, oatcakes would have been baked on a flat iron girdle, hung over the fire at The Three Chimneys. Eaten with crowdie cheese, also homemade on most crofts in days gone by, or spread with local honey, oatcakes remain a great favourite with every nationality that visits us in Skye.

I add oatmeal to my wholemeal bread, giving it added texture. I've

added toasted oatmeal and whisky to ice cream and use it with rolled oats in fruit crumble toppings, biscuits and scones. Cranachan made with fresh double cream, whipped together with toasted oatmeal, honey and whisky and served with fresh summer berries, is quite the best pudding in the world. Haggis is another of Scotland's national dishes, a delicious combination of sheep's offal mixed with seasoned oatmeal. Few things could be finer than herring fillets dipped in oatmeal before frying gently in butter. This simple, Scottish way of serving fish is unique to our culinary heritage, and Tatties and Herring is typical of traditional dishes that I believe we should be more proud of.

Skirlie (so-called because the sound of the fat melting in a very hot frying pan is supposed to resemble the skirl of the bagpipes!) can be used in a variety of ways. Have a go at making Skirlie to stuff your roast chicken on Sunday. Use the carcass to make some chicken stock the next day and enhance the Oatmeal and Potato Soup recipe. Use the Skirlie idea to make Skirlie Mash and then, use the mash to make Skirlie Potato Cakes, delicious with any roast meats.

Brose is a mixture of oatmeal, water, salt and butter. These ingredients are basic constituents of my recipe for Mussel Brose, a hearty soup that is a great favourite in the restaurant. The addition of oatmeal creates a unique flavour and texture to the more classic methods frequently used to cook mussels.

And when you are cooking with oats or oatmeal, don't forget to stir the mealy pot clockwise, for a measure of good luck!

Oatmeal and Potato Soup

During the years 2000/01, I contributed to a number of programmes on Scottish radio. 'Scottish Connections' was broadcast live from the BBC's Inverness studio. It was strange cooking on the radio, knowing that the listeners could not watch what I was doing. The radio 'kitchen' was a poor relation to the swish kitchen sets built for television studios and the many popular TV cookery programmes that appear on our screens, featuring celebrity chefs. It consisted of a trestle table, an electric ring and a few utensils. I would pack the car early in the morning and make the 3-hour drive to Inverness in time to perform live on radio late-morning. I loved doing this. It was great fun and I had a good rapport with the presenter Mark Stevens. One week I was asked for soup recipes to cheer up the nation suffering from an epidemic of colds and 'flu. I cooked Oatmeal and Potato Soup on the programme and they received their biggest ever post bag requesting a copy of the recipe.

INGREDIENTS:

600g potatoes, weighed when peeled and diced. Choose a floury potato that is good for mash.

300g onions, weighed when peeled and chopped quite small.

50g slightly salted butter.

2 rounded tbsp medium oatmeal.

1 generous litre vegetable or chicken stock.

Approximately 300ml fresh milk plus 120ml double cream.

Freshly ground sea salt, black pepper and grated whole nutmeg.

Freshly chopped chives for garnish.

METHOD:

Melt butter in a large saucepan until foamy. **Add** onions and turn in butter and cook until softened. **Add** potatoes and stir together with onion. **Add** salt and black pepper. **Allow** to cook gently for a few minutes. **Pour** in stock, bring to boil and then simmer with lid on, for at least 20–30 minutes. **Add** oatmeal, stir and simmer for further 10 minutes. **Add** milk and liquidise. **Reheat** and finish with cream, more seasoning if necessary and some freshly grated whole nutmeg. **Serve** immediately with garnish of freshly chopped chives. **If** too thick, add a little more milk or cream. **Serve** immediately, as the longer this soup is left to stand, the thicker it becomes because of the oatmeal.

If using chicken stock and adding cooked chicken pieces at the end, make sure soup is heated thoroughly. **Add** some finely chopped leeks with the chopped onion, at the beginning, for a further variation.

STAGE ONE. COOKING THE MUSSELS.

INGREDIENTS:

Wash and de-beard 1kg mussels. Discard any that are cracked or open.

50g slightly salted butter.

1 medium onion, finely chopped.

2 large cloves garlic, finely chopped.

1 heaped tbsp chopped parsley.

Freshly ground black pepper.

200ml dry white wine.

100ml water.

METHOD:

Melt the butter in a large pan. **You** will need a good lid to fit the pan. **Soften** the onion and garlic in the hot butter. **Stir** in the parsley and add some freshly ground black pepper. **Pour** in the wine and water and bring to the boil. **Add** all the mussels, lower the heat, cover with close-fitting lid and leave to steam until mussels have opened. (**If** you want to serve mussels traditionally, cook them to this stage and serve them in warm bowls with the cooking liquor poured over them. **Sprinkle** with extra chopped parsley and chives when serving.) **Remove** the mussels using a slotted spoon and leave on a large dish to cool. **Strain** the cooking liquor through a fine sieve and reserve. **Rinse** out saucepan.

STAGE TWO. MAKING THE BROSE.

INGREDIENTS:

500g potatoes, weighed when peeled and diced. Choose a floury variety that is good for mash.

200g onion, weighed when peeled and chopped quite small.

50g slightly salted butter.

2 rounded tbsp medium oatmeal.

Approximately 250ml fresh milk plus 150ml double cream.

Freshly ground sea salt, black pepper, chopped chives and parsley, to finish.

METHOD:

Melt the butter until hot and foamy. **Add** onions and cook until soft. **Add** potatoes and stir together with the onion. **Allow** to cook gently for a few minutes. **Pour** in the strained mussel liquor. **Bring** to boil and then simmer with the lid on for at least 20–30 minutes. **Add** oatmeal, stir and simmer for a further 5–10 minutes. **Meanwhile**, remove the cooled mussels from their shells and reserve in a bowl. **Retain** a few whole for garnish. **When** Brose is cooked, add fresh milk and liquidise. **Stir** in shelled mussels and the double cream. **Reheat** and season to taste. **Be** careful, as salt may not be necessary. **Adjust** the thickness of the Brose at this stage. **You** may need to add a little more cream or a dash of white wine and water. **Finish** with freshly chopped chives and parsley stirred through the Brose. **Serve** hot in warmed bowls with whole mussels placed on top for garnish.

Some freshly baked wholemeal bread and salad would be good to serve with this soup, for a meal-in-one.

Skirlie

Traditionally, Skirlie was made with suet. It would have been served on its own, hot, with boiled potatoes. I like to add finely chopped parsley and chives, shape it into balls about the size of a golf ball and place them around the chicken while roasting. In recent years, chefs have been flavouring mashed potato in all sorts of ways. I hit upon the idea of making Skirlie Mash using the same ingredients. It has been a huge success. The mash has now been adapted to become Skirlie Potato Cakes that we serve with venison. That's what happens in kitchens!

Once upon a time, Highlanders made their own particular brand of haggis using venison with seasoned oatmeal.

INGREDIENTS AND METHOD:

Melt 50g of slightly salted butter until hot and foamy in a hot frying pan.

Stir in 200g of very finely chopped onion and fry until just turning brown. (Can you hear the skirl?)

Add 150g medium oatmeal and stir together well.

Allow to cook gently for a few minutes.

Season with freshly ground sea salt and black pepper, as required.

Add fresh herbs if using.

TO MAKE SKIRLIE MASH:

Boil approximately 1kg floury potatoes (weighed when peeled) and mash when cooked. **Stir** in Skirlie mixture while it is still warm. **The** butter in the Skirlie should be sufficient to give a good texture and flavour, but if you need to add a little more, do so to suit your taste. **Check** for seasoning before serving. **This** is great with game stews and hotpots, or roast chicken dishes.

TO MAKE SKIRLIE POTATO CAKES:

Use the Skirlie Mash mixture and shape it into cakes, approximately 8cm round, by 2cm deep. **Brush** with melted butter and bake on a buttered baking tray on the top shelf of a hot oven for 10 minutes before serving. **They** should be nut brown and crisp on the outside, but soft and warm in the middle. **The** cakes could be frozen and baked before serving, in which case, allow about 20 minutes on the top shelf of a very hot oven.

The Skirlie Potato Cakes in the photograph are served with Venison Collops-in-the-Pan and lightly cooked Savoy cabbage flavoured with juniper berries. The sauce is a rich game gravy made with prunes and bitter chocolate.

Grilled West Coast Cod and Skirlie Mash in Saffron Broth
with Mussels, Leek and Fennel

I cooked this recipe on 'Desert Island Chefs', a programme produced by Grampian Television and shown throughout Scotland in April 2002. The film crew seemed to take over The Three Chimneys for two days in March and it was a hectic schedule. I enjoyed the experience, but I don't think I'm cut out to be a TV chef! The ingredients below should be sufficient for 4 people. I suggest that you prepare this dish in the following order of work:

1. Prepare the mussels and set aside.

2. Reduce the mussel liquor for the sauce while you:

3. Prepare the skirlie.

4. Prepare the mash.

5. Prepare the leek and fennel for the sauce.

6. While you boil the potatoes, prepare the fish ready for grilling, cover and set aside.

7. Finish the skirlie mash, cover in a heatproof dish and keep warm, while you:

8. Finish the sauce and keep it warm, while you:

9. Grill the cod.

10. Assemble the dish and serve.

THE MUSSEL AND SAFFRON BROTH:

In addition to the ingredients required for cooking the mussels as in the recipe for Mussel Brose, you will need:

Approximately 400ml of double cream.

A large pinch of saffron threads.

METHOD:

Prepare and cook the mussels as for Mussel Brose in previous recipe. When you remove the mussels with a slotted spoon and place them on a large dish, strain the liquor into a smaller saucepan. Heat the liquor until boiling. Reduce the liquor until you have 100ml of liquid. Add enough double cream to make the amount up to 500ml. Stir in the saffron threads, crumbling them lightly, but not completely.

THE SKIRLIE MASH:

Prepare the Skirlie Mash as in the previous recipe, cover with foil and keep in a warm place until ready to serve.

THE FISH:

4 x 175g pieces of fresh cod fillet, skin on.

50g butter – unsalted is better.

A squeeze of lemon juice.

Freshly ground sea salt and white pepper.

Line a baking tray with foil. Brush with melted butter, season and squeeze a little lemon juice over the butter. Place the cod on the tray, spaced apart. Season each piece of cod with salt and pepper, add a squeeze of lemon juice on top and a good knob of butter. Cover and set aside until ready to cook. Cook, without turning over, under a hot grill for approximately 5 minutes. Remove from heat, brush with a little more butter and keep in a warm place until ready to finish off under the grill and serve.

TO FINISH THE SAFFRON BROTH:

Set aside 16 mussels in the shell for garnish. **Remove** the mussel meat from the remaining shells and set aside. **Finely** chop 1 small bulb, or half a large bulb of fennel. **Finely** chop the white of half a leek. **Melt** 25g of unsalted butter and cook the leek and fennel gently until it is beginning to go soft. **Stir** in the saffron sauce and mix together. **Leave** over a gentle heat allowing the sauce to heat thoroughly, reduce and thicken a little more. **It** will also turn more yellow in colour as it heats through.

A minute or two before you are ready to assemble the dish, add the mussels and warm through gently. **The** mussels will become rubbery if overcooked.

TO ASSEMBLE THE DISH:

Place the skirlie mash in the centre of the warm serving plate or dish. **Spoon** the mussel and saffron broth around the mash, but not over it. **Put** the cooked cod on top of the mash. **Place** the mussels in the shell around the fish to garnish. **Serve** immediately.

THE THREE CHIMNEYS was closed from November to March every year until the winter of 1998/99. This was when we built our new bedroom accommodation in The House Over-By and refurbished the interior of the restaurant in the original building, to include a snug bar. In earlier years, we turned the restaurant dining rooms back into our family sitting room, lit the fire every day, closed the curtains when it grew dark and watched TV. Our winter evenings could not have been more different from the hectic life we lived throughout the months of the tourist season.

Summer visitors to Skye love being away from it all when they are here on holiday. However, they often say they would not survive living here all year round, so far from 'civilisation'. They can see how preoccupied we are running the restaurant, but in the past, they could never understand how we coped with life when The Three Chimneys was closed.

"What do you do in the winter?" was a frequently asked question.

"Lead a normal life," was my immediate reply.

I cooked family suppers, helped with homework, did the ironing, went shopping, spent an evening with friends – did ordinary things!

After our two-week holiday, a family Christmas and the New Year celebrations, there was not much time left before March when the restaurant reopened. A great deal of work was done during the earlier winter months in preparation for the busier times ahead, but we also enjoyed the fun side of a social life at this time of year. Visitors are wrong to think there is no night-life in Skye. The Three Chimneys was a great place for one of many parties.

The long workbench in the kitchen served us well as our buffet table and the double draining boards made a perfect bar. With plenty of space for dancing, the stone walls resounded to loud music, laughter and lively conversation until the wee small hours.

The early months of the year were always the worst for us financially. We had no income, just a large overdraft, and were constantly under pressure from the Bank not to exceed it. This was also hard! We sailed very close to bankruptcy on several occasions. These were scary years because The Three Chimneys was also our home. If we lost the restaurant, we lost everything.

We soon came to realise that the days of running a small, tourism-related, way of life, seasonal business in the Highlands could not last forever. Our annual overheads were high and rarely matched our low profit margins.

We fought back every year, but were often made to feel we were the only people who had any faith in The Three Chimneys as a business. We knew we needed to build bedrooms and somehow market ourselves as an all year round destination experience. In remote north-west Skye? It was a marketing man's nightmare!

Our business life was not exactly a piece of cake. There was definitely no icing on it. From the mid-80s to the late-90s, we fought against occasional local maliciousness, attempted fish farming developments on our doorstep and a dyed-in-the-wool attitude towards the value of the tourism industry to the local economy. Worst of all were the men in grey suits in the Bank's head office, who had no idea or understanding of what we were managing to achieve. They were so hard. There was no leeway. Ironically, we lived through it using credit cards.

Every March we bounced back into business, with brave hearts and optimism for the coming months. One year we decided to refresh the face of The Three Chimneys with a new colour scheme and soft furnishings to match. As the Bank would not allow us any extra money, we opened an account at John Lewis. We bought paint, paper, carpets and curtains. Eddie painted and decorated, while I prepared new menus, revamped our graphics and planned mini-marketing campaigns locally to off-set the 'low' months. Our new look created great interest and gave us the boost we needed to revive business for another year.

Looking back, I realise that some of the media coverage we have received in recent years would have been even more useful during the 90s. Not until we launched The House Over-By and gained 5-stars for the Highlands, were we ever independently 'reviewed' by a restaurant critic.

We survived by the skin of our teeth. But we survived to tell the tale.

The
golden
preserve
of Scottish
kitchens

IF EVER my children are famous enough to be on BBC Radio 4's 'Desert Island Discs', I will not be surprised if they choose a piece of music that reminds them of their childhood days in Skye and the trauma of living with their Mum making endless jars of marmalade for hours on end in the winter. I can feel the Guilty Mother Complex creeping over me at the thought of it. They even reminded me recently of the time I had gallantly soldiered on with the job by candlelight, throughout a two day power cut. It was complete marmalade madness!

Having left home in the morning to the sound of me putting yet more glass jars to warm in the oven, the children would arrive home to the wonderful smell of marmalade on a fast rolling boil, wafting through the back door from the steaming hot pans on the stove. Piles of scrubbed oranges and lemons lay all around the kitchen, together with bag upon bag of sugar. There would be peel stacked for chopping, pips and pulp ready to boil up for their pectin, juice straining and marmalade setting before being ladled into the ranks of spotless, warm jars. In short, the whole of the restaurant kitchen became a veritable jam factory for a few days in February. And it was all in order to make enough marmalade to keep us in Hot Marmalade Pudding for the rest of the year.

I love marmalade as much as I have always loved the story of

Janet Keiller of Dundee and the cargo of bitter oranges bought by her husband James from a storm-bound Spanish ship. They were so sour, the Keillers could not sell them in their shop and so Janet set about turning them into jam. Little did she know she had invented something so unique that it would revolutionise the world of breakfast throughout the land. Yet another great Scottish invention – probably one of the best!

There are many types of marmalade using combinations of all the different citrus fruits, besides the traditional Seville orange variety. However, the bitter-sharp flavour of Sevilles that continue to arrive from Spain in January and February, is what makes 'proper' home-made marmalade taste so good. There is also a myriad number of recipes and methods for making marmalade, many handed down through the family for generations. I have used the following recipe for almost twenty years with great success. Keep the peel quite chunky, but not too thick, and always include the lemon peel too.

Seville oranges are impossible to eat as a fruit, but their zesty, tangy flavour is a unique addition to a whole range of savoury sauces I have made to accompany dishes as diverse as roast ham or wild duck, to fresh cod or king scallops. Like all good things, the simplest are the best – think of toast and marmalade! I've used marmalade to make Caledonian ice cream and I always put a spoonful in fruit cakes and bread pudding. When I roast a gammon joint for breakfast at Christmas, I glaze it with mustard and marmalade. A hollandaise-style sauce made with the rind and juice of Seville oranges instead of lemons, is superb with white fish. Then, of course, there is the

legendary Hot Marmalade Pudding, reputed to attract customers from all over the world to our remote corner of north-west Skye. An old-fashioned, simple steamed pudding, it is so popular that it has never been off the menu since we first opened the restaurant.

I cannot imagine how many jars of marmalade I must have filled, sealed and stored away in my life. It is traditional to add a splash of whisky to home-made marmalade, and the secret of my own, of course, is Talisker, the golden spirit of Skye. Just two teaspoonfuls carefully stirred into a hot jar of freshly potted marmalade make the perfect addition to the golden preserve of Scottish kitchens.

Making home-made marmalade is part of Scotland's culinary heritage and definitely one tradition we must keep alive. If you have never tried and tasted home-made marmalade before, I can promise you, your life will never be quite the same again!

Three Chimneys Traditional Marmalade

I have made marmalade with this recipe for years and years. It is a good method when making bulk supplies. I could not resist leaving the quantities in pounds and pints, just for old times' sake. I'll never get used to metric measures! Of course, we now have another reason to make marmalade – for breakfast for our guests in The House Over-By.

INGREDIENTS:

4lb (approximately 2kg) of Seville oranges.

4 lemons.

8 pints (approximately 4litres) water.

8 lb (approximately 4kg) granulated sugar.

METHOD:

Put the whole fruit in a basin of very lukewarm water and give them a good wash and a gentle scrub. **Put** the washed fruit, whole, into a large saucepan or preserving pan. **Add** the water and put the lid on. **Bring** to the boil and simmer for about one-and-a-half hours. **You** should be able to easily pierce the skins of the fruit with a skewer when they are ready. **Remove** the fruit from the water and place on a large dish to cool down a little. **With** a sharp knife, cut the cooked fruit into quarters and scrape out the pulp and pips. **Add** the pips, the pulp and any obvious residual juice into the pan with the water that was used to boil the fruit. **Boil** the pips and pulp for a full 10 minutes and then strain. **Retain** the juice, but discard the strained pulp and pips. **Meanwhile**, put the sugar in a large container, roasting tin or bowl and put it into a low oven to warm through. **This** will make it easier for the sugar to dissolve. **Put** your clean jam jars into the low oven to warm through ready for potting the marmalade. **Chop** or slice the orange and lemon peel to your favourite size and shape. **Put** the chopped peel into the reserved

water. **Bring** to the boil. **Add** the warm sugar. **Stir** over a gentle heat until you are sure that all the sugar is dissolved. **Bring** this mixture to the boil and continue to boil rapidly without stirring for approximately half an hour. **You** are aiming to reach setting point. (See below.) **Leave** the marmalade in the hot pan for a short time until it shows that it is beginning to set properly. **The** peel will be showing signs of becoming 'suspended' in the mixture. **Carefully** ladle the hot marmalade into warm, clean jam jars. **These** should have been warmed up in a low oven for at least 30 minutes beforehand. **Seal** the finished jars. (Makes about 6 kg) **Enjoy** using it!

TO TEST FOR SETTING POINT:

Put a small spoonful of cooked marmalade onto a very cold saucer. (**Keep** a few at the ready in the fridge or freezer.) **Allow** it to cool a little and then push it with your finger, or tilt the dish to one side. **If** the marmalade wrinkles up, it is ready.

The Famous Hot Marmalade Pudding

I first experimented with this pudding long before we moved to Skye and took over the restaurant. I decided to make it for my late, very dear father-in-law, John Spear, for his 74th birthday. He had complained to me that nobody made steamed puddings any more and I resolved to make him one instead of a birthday cake. The original recipe was in a small, paperback cookbook that I found in my local Sainsbury's in West Wickham! I adapted it, of course, but it goes to prove that there is nothing new under the sun in the way of recipes. Someone, somewhere, will have created something very similar, at some time before you!

Several years later, when we took over The Three Chimneys, I wanted to put a traditional 'nursery' pudding on the menu and dug out the recipe. It has since become a signature dish and has remained on the menu since the very first night. Some people imagine a stodgy suet pudding with a dollop of marmalade at the bottom of the basin. In fact it is very light as there is so little flour in the recipe and it is full of flavour. The marmalade is combined throughout, giving the dessert a rich, amber colour. The two hour steaming is essential to its success.

INGREDIENTS:

150g fine brown breadcrumbs.

120g soft light brown sugar.

25g self-raising wholemeal flour (white self-raising would do).

120g fresh butter, plus extra for greasing the bowl.

8 tbsp well-flavoured, coarse-cut marmalade (home-made is always the best).

3 large eggs.

1 rounded tsp bicarbonate of soda plus 1 tbsp water to mix.

METHOD:

Butter a 3 pint pudding basin well. **Place** the breadcrumbs, flour and sugar in a large mixing bowl. **Melt** the butter together with the marmalade, in a saucepan over a gentle heat. **Pour** the melted ingredients over the dry ingredients and mix together thoroughly. **Whisk** the eggs until frothy and beat gently into the mixture until blended together well. **Last** of all, dissolve the bicarbonate of soda in 1 tablespoonful of cold water. **Stir** this into the pudding mixture, which will increase in volume as it absorbs the bicarbonate of soda. **Spoon** the mixture into the prepared basin. **Cover** it with a close-fitting lid, or alternatively, make a lid with circles of buttered greaseproof paper and foil, pleated together across the centre and tied securely around the rim of the basin. **Place** the pudding basin in a saucepan of boiling water. **The** water should reach halfway up the side of the basin. **Cover** the pan with a close-fitting lid and simmer the pudding for 2 hours. **The** water will need topping up throughout the cooking period. **Turn** out on to a serving dish, slice and serve hot, with fresh cream, ice cream, or – as we do at The Three Chimneys – with Drambuie Custard.

Drambuie Custard

This is a proper egg custard flavoured with Drambuie liqueur. It is served warm, poured around the pudding. Alternatively, other flavours could be added, such as vanilla, ginger or crushed cardamom, if you prefer. A tablespoonful of fresh ground coffee can be added, which is delicious with hot or cold chocolate desserts.

INGREDIENTS:

275ml fresh milk.

275ml fresh double cream.

6 egg yolks.

100g caster sugar.

2 tbsp Drambuie liqueur.

Whisk the egg yolks together with the sugar until pale, slightly thick and creamy. **Gently** warm the milk and cream until it is just beginning to bubble. **Pour** the milk and cream onto the egg and sugar mixture and whisk together. **Return** the mixture to the saucepan. **Bring** to the boil very slowly, stirring all the time. **As** soon as it begins to thicken, or coats the back of the wooden spoon, remove from the heat and pour into a bowl or jug for serving. **Stir** in the Drambuie, or flavouring of your choice. **Serve** immediately. **Alternatively**, cool the custard quickly in a bowl sitting on ice and refrigerate when cold, until required. **The** custard can be used cold for assembling a trifle, serving with frozen or chilled desserts, or reheated carefully for serving with a hot pudding.

Whisky Fruit Loaf

We serve this with afternoon tea to welcome guests staying at The House Over-By. Jean Ferguson, who lives nearby The Three Chimneys, gave the recipe to me. Jean also cut the ribbon when we officially opened The House Over-By. She is in her eighties now and has many fascinating tales to tell of her island life in Raasay and Skye. When she was young she cooked in a number of the grander Skye houses and Highland shooting lodges.

INGREDIENTS:

170g raisins.

170g sultanas.

140g currants.

250ml water.

115g butter.

140g soft dark brown sugar.

3 eggs, beaten.

280g self-raising flour.

2 tsp mixed ground spice.

2 heaped tbsp marmalade.

30g nibbed almonds.

115g chopped glacé cherries.

115g chopped mixed peel.

3 tbsp whisky.

METHOD:

Grease 2 x 2lb loaf tins with a little butter and line with parchment paper. **Put** the raisins, sultanas, currants, water, butter and brown sugar into a large saucepan. **Heat** slowly until the butter has melted completely. **Take** the pan off the heat and allow to cool down for a few minutes. **Add** the beaten eggs, sieved flour, spice, marmalade, cherries, peel, almonds and whisky. **Mix** thoroughly. **Pour** mixture into the prepared loaf tins. **Bake** for 1 hour (Gas Mark 4, 180°C, 350°F). **The** finished cake should be a deep golden brown. **Cool** in the loaf tins for at least 30 minutes before turning on to a wire tray to cool completely. **Store** in an airtight tin until ready to use. **This** fruit loaf also freezes very well.

FOR MANY *years we ran a Whisky Shop in the ground floor room next door to the restaurant that has now become the Bar. This was one of our various attempts over the years to make the business more viable. We also imagined it would give us some earnings over the penniless winter months.*

Looking back, there were few places on the island where one could buy a souvenir bottle of malt to take home, and at first the shop was an enormous success. We tentatively put some unusual bottles on the shelves, some of which were quite rare and expensive. We also included some very old Taliskers from Skye's only distillery. They sold like hot cakes! We could hardly believe it. Over the first summer season we sold more cases of Scottish country wines made by the Moniack Winery than any other retail outlet. (A statistic Eddie would prefer me not to record!)

Alas, as the years ensued, many more outlets began to stock whisky on their shelves, and the distillery industry itself became much more marketing-conscious. It became harder and harder to compete on price as we were buying in such small quantities, and eventually the shop became a liability rather than an asset.

I used to make enough marmalade to sell in the shop too. I also made coarse-grain whisky mustard and a variety of chutneys. It was time-consuming for very little return. I would label each jar by hand and cut cloth lid covers from pretty fabrics. This kind of cottage industry is fun to an extent, but hardly worth it financially. Even buying jam jars with sealable screw-top lids was uneconomic in small quantities. Sourcing them in the first place was a major task in itself. These were all winter jobs.

For a few years we sold take-away picnic lunches through the shop, popular with people on their way to Neist Point for a walk, or simply bought because we could not accommodate them for a meal in the restaurant. I cannot remember how I coped with these orders on top of those coming in from the dining rooms. We were so busy! It must have been mayhem!

We also tried to promote the shop at Christmas for the first two years, selling a number of food items such as our shortbread and chocolate brandy fudge cake. I made Christmas cakes and puddings to order. Of course, everything was beautifully packaged with the help of the pinking shears, festive ribbon and labels – usually by myself, at 3 o'clock in the morning.

On reflection, we learned the hard way. After a few years sales were dropping off, by which time Talisker Distillery had a shop within its own, brand new Visitor Centre, Dunvegan Castle was selling its own souvenir label and the local Co-Op had expanded its range enormously. Closing down was a huge relief to us, although it had been fun in other ways. And we learned a lot about whisky!

Under Bracadale skies

WHEN YOU arrive in Skye and take the main road up the western side of the island, your journey at first takes you over a wild stretch of moorland. The Cuillin Mountains are behind you and the long road winds its way into the distance. You emerge at the other end around a wide sweeping bend. The view out to sea and beyond, to The Minch and the Outer Hebrides, is breathtaking. This is Bracadale – home to spectacular skies – and to the big brown crab.

Loch Harport sweeps out to sea between the steep sides of Bracadale Point and the lighthouse on the tip of Portnalong. The deep inlet of Loch Beag provides a natural harbour for boats moored by the jetty at Struan. To the north-west, the flat tops of MacLeod's Tables soar high above. Whatever the time of day, or the time of year, you will be as spellbound by this vista as I always am.

If you pull in at the roadside, you may catch sight of one or two creel fishing boats busy in the loch, or setting out to explore the rocky Skye coastline further, into The Minch and around Rum and Canna. Fishermen seem to have a 'love-hate' relationship with the sea. At times their work is totally addictive, and yet, they can be driven to the depths of despondency

when they hit a bad spell. Dealing with their fragile feelings can sometimes be difficult, as I well know!

For whilst some women hanker after a 'man with a van that can', my life as a Skye chef is spent chasing 'a man with creels that deals'. One such Sgitheanach of infamous distinction, is known locally as Donnie Dangerous, partly because he dares to fish single-handedly in areas where no-one

else risks going. There has been many a summer's night when the phone has rung in our hot and hectic kitchen. "Hi! It's Donnie here. I'm just passing the lighthouse at Portnalong. It's a lovely sunset out here. How many lobsters do you want?"

Frazzled by the heat of the grill, it is not hard to imagine anything better, at that point in time, than being out at sea in a boat with a gentle breeze blowing through your hair. But a fisherman's life is not often as idyllic. These guys work hard – long hours, in all weathers. An hour or so later, Donnie turns up with a crate full of blue beauties. And the late night boiling rigmarole begins all over again...

Fishing runs in families in these parts. My other main man, Willie Murdo, sets out from Dunvegan Pier. He takes his creel boat far out into The Minch to catch superb langoustines from the deep water channel that runs through this narrow stretch of water between Skye and the Outer Hebrides. I suspect that both men have been to sea with their fathers and grandfathers since they were big enough to wear wellies. Both men have played a huge part in The Three Chimneys success story.

Donnie and Willie Murdo land brown crab too. Boiling and shelling them is time-consuming on a large scale. I was, therefore, delighted when another enterprising local set up a small 'factory' unit nearby for the sole purpose of producing top quality, fresh crabmeat. Rick The Crab has become another of my heroes. His crabmeat is prepared with the utmost care.

The fishermen land their fresh catch, live. Rick cooks it and produces the finished goods. It is yet another local product that Skye can boast to the world about. City chefs are very envious of my local supplies.

Of course, I take delivery of whole brown crabs and little velvet crabs too. I need the whole crab (Partan in Gaelic) for its shell with which I make our crab stock. The stock is essential in Partan Bree (Crab Bisque) and is also an excellent ingredient in our Crab Risotto. Hot Crab Tart is made with the fresh crabmeat and has appeared on our menu at The Three Chimneys in various guises since our opening night – but that's another story!

A quality fishmonger should have good fresh crabmeat for sale, or he

will obtain it for you if you order it in advance. If you are buying whole crab, it should be live and smell fresh, with no hint of ammonia. If it is good and meaty, it should feel heavy in your hand. Both claws should be intact. Male crabs have a higher content of white meat than female crabs as they have bigger claws. The brown meat in the female crab can be particularly thick and creamy with the addition of the coral pink roe.

If you are preparing crab yourself, take care to remove the 'dead man's fingers' which are the gills, found around the edge of the centre section. These are easy to distinguish. They are creamy coloured and look like small feathery ferns. If you are careful to keep the main part of the crab shell intact, you can wash it thoroughly and pack the prepared meat back into it. You would normally identify this presentation as being Dressed Crab. The shell can also be used for Partan Pie and is strong enough to withstand the heat of the grill or the oven when browning the top, to finish it off.

Bracadale Crab Tart

A small portion of this tart could be served on its own as a starter, or a larger slice as a main course.
We make individual ones for the restaurant and serve them with Warm Cherry Tomato Vinaigrette.

TO START WITH:

Pre-heat the oven to Gas Mark 5 (190°C or 375°F).

Place a flat baking sheet on centre shelf to warm.

Grease a 25cm wide x 5cm deep flan tin and line with

shortcrust pastry.

Place flan tin on top of baking sheet and bake blind.

INGREDIENTS FOR THE FILLING:

Approx 250g fresh, mixed (brown and white) crabmeat.

Juice of half a lemon.

2 tbsp tomato passata (or 1 tbsp tomato puree).

1 tbsp cream sherry.

1 tbsp freshly chopped parsley.

Freshly ground sea salt and white pepper.

2 whole eggs + 2 egg yolks.

125ml (small carton) fresh double cream.

1 heaped tbsp freshly grated Parmesan cheese.

METHOD:

Whisk the eggs, egg yolks and cream together in mixing bowl.
Add the crabmeat together with all the other ingredients,
except cheese. **Season** with salt and pepper. **Mix** thoroughly
and pour into prepared flan case. **Sprinkle** with freshly grated
Parmesan cheese and return to hot oven to bake for
25–30 minutes until surface is slightly risen and firm to
touch and turning golden in colour.

Cherry Tomato Vinaigrette

INGREDIENTS:

25–30 ripe cherry tomatoes, washed and cut into halves.

1 tbsp sherry vinegar.

2 tbsp good quality tomato passata.

1 clove garlic, crushed.

Freshly ground sea salt and white pepper.

6 tbsp good quality olive oil (or preferably, olive oil

infused with basil).

METHOD:

Put all ingredients except olive oil into blender and liquidise as smooth as possible. **Sieve** the tomato mixture through a fine mesh sieve into a bowl. **Rinse** the blender goblet to remove all traces of pips and small fragments of tomato skin. **Return** the sieved mixture to the clean goblet. **Remove** the cap from the centre of the lid of the blender. **Switch** on the blender and pour the olive oil through the top in a steady stream, until all is absorbed into the tomato mixture. **Check** seasoning and refrigerate before use. **Alternatively**, gently warm the vinaigrette before serving with the hot crab tart. **Serve** the tart with a little basil leaf salad to garnish. **Lemon** basil is perfect if you can grow your own.

Partan Bree

INGREDIENTS FOR THE CRAB STOCK:

The shells from 2 large brown crabs, cooked and meat removed. Meat should yield approximately 500g. Reserve the meat for crab recipes.

1 large onion, roughly sliced.

1 small piece of fennel, with feathery tops and some celery leaves, roughly chopped.

Sprigs of parsley with stalk, broken up.

Half a lemon, sliced.

2 bay leaves.

1 tsp whole white peppercorns.

2 tbsp brandy.

50g butter.

STAGE 1:

Put the crab shells in a roasting tin and place on the top shelf of a hot oven for 20 minutes, to roast. **Remove** from oven when dry and brittle. **Break** into smaller pieces with the end of a rolling pin.

STAGE 2:

Melt the butter in a large saucepan until hot and foamy. **Add** all the vegetables, lemon, herbs and peppercorns and soften in the hot butter. **Add** roasted shells and stir well, continually breaking up. **Flame** with brandy. **Cover** with approximately 1.5 litres of cold water, bring to the boil and simmer for up to 1 hour. **Strain** through a colander, and then strain liquid a second time, through a fine sieve. **Reserve** for soup or risotto, or freeze in batches.

INGREDIENTS FOR THE CRAB BISQUE:

STAGE 1:

1 large onion, finely chopped.

50g long grain white rice.

50g butter.

Finely grated rind of 1 lemon.

Sea salt and freshly ground white pepper.

750ml crab stock.

Melt butter in saucepan until hot and foamy, add onion and cook until soft. **Add** rice, lemon, salt and pepper and stir together well. **Pour** in stock. **Bring** to boil and then simmer for 20 minutes. **Liquidise** and return to pot.

STAGE 2:

Add the following:

150ml milk.

4 tbsp of Madeira or cream sherry.

Juice of half a lemon.

1 scant tbsp tomato passata.

Large pinch of paprika.

2 tbsp finely chopped herbs – a mixture of chervil, flat parsley and fennel is great.

250g mixed brown and white crabmeat.

Stir all ingredients together well. **Check** seasoning. **Adjust** texture with a little cream if necessary. **Serve** in warmed bowls with home-baked wholemeal bread.

Skye Crab Risotto

To complete all 3 stages of this recipe, you will need 250g white crabmeat and 250g brown crabmeat.

INGREDIENTS FOR THE RISOTTO:

200g arborio rice.

Zest of 1 lime, plus juice.

The white and pale green of 2 large spring onions, very finely chopped.

1 medium red chilli (not too hot) de-seeded and very finely chopped.

1 clove of garlic, crushed.

2 tbsp fresh coriander, finely chopped.

2 tbsp freshly grated Parmesan.

Freshly ground sea salt and white pepper.

450ml hot crab stock, made up to 750ml with a mixture of white wine and water. (Liquid must be hot when pouring into rice.)

125g white crabmeat.

2 tbsp good olive oil.

METHOD:

Line a cake tin, approximately 20cm square and 5cm deep, with baking parchment paper. **Heat** olive oil in a large saucepan, or preferably, a wide, deep frying pan. **Stir** lime zest, spring onion, chilli and garlic in hot oil until beginning to soften. **Add** the rice and stir well to coat with oil. **Pour** in one third of hot stock mixture and stir well. **Allow** rice to absorb the liquid. **This** will take approximately 10 minutes. **Keep** adding hot stock mixture until rice is cooked al dente, fluffy in appearance and no longer absorbing more liquid easily. **Add** crab to rice and heat through thoroughly. **Check** for seasoning and add lime juice to taste, if required. **Remove** from heat and stir in Parmesan cheese and

coriander. **Pack** the risotto mixture into the lined cake tin evenly. **Leave** to chill in the refrigerator, preferably overnight. **Cut** round shapes with a 5cm pastry cutter before serving.

INGREDIENTS FOR THE CRAB TOPPING:

125g white crabmeat.

125g brown crabmeat.

Juice of 2 limes.

1 tsp good quality mayonnaise.

Freshly ground sea salt and white pepper to taste.

Mix all together, cover and refrigerate before use.

INGREDIENTS FOR THE DRESSING:

125g brown crabmeat.

125g thick Greek-style yoghurt.

2 tsp good quality tomato passata.

2 tsp lemon juice.

Freshly ground sea salt and white pepper to taste.

Put crabmeat, yoghurt and tomato passata in blender and liquidise until smooth. **Season** with salt and white pepper and lemon juice to taste.

TO ASSEMBLE THE DISH:

Drizzle dressing over plate. **Place** crab risotto shape on top. **Pile** mixture of crabmeat on top of risotto. **Garnish** with fresh coriander and serve with salad leaves dressed with lemon juice and olive oil.

I CANNOT write about crab without telling the tale of our very first night running The Three Chimneys, April 1985. It was chaos. I nearly ran away in the middle of it all, sickening deep inside as I quizzed myself over why I ever imagined I could do the job at all.

Despite the previous few months of planning and organising, we were not 'ready' on our opening night. Two local women, both about my own age, with same-age children, were our waitresses. Anne Gracie and Catriona Oliver had both worked for the previous owner. They arrived for work at the appointed hour in their 'new' outfits and were, very obviously, aghast at my state of disarray. I know this because they were whispering to each other in Gaelic – something they would never

do normally, as I realised as our friendship grew over the years. Thankfully, they had more experience than I had and swung into action, setting tables, organising coffee cups and making up salads just as they had always done.

Meanwhile I scurried about in a frenzy. We had a comfortable 16 covers booked until about 4.30pm when Eddie went off to Dunvegan to the offices of a small local company, Gaeltec, to photocopy my typewritten menu. (No word processors or computers in those days! We did not even have a fax.) When he returned he had accrued a few more bookings from well-meaning, supportive locals. Our numbers had shot up to 32. I was on my own in the kitchen without a single idea of how I was going to cope and absolutely no experience to draw upon. Worse still, virtually everyone was booked to arrive at 8 o'clock. As we neared the

official opening time, there were people knocking on the door trying to book a last-minute table – and one man knocking on the door trying to deliver a table we had been awaiting for some weeks.

All of the dishes I had so carefully planned and practised, began to go wrong. The Soup Lorraine would not thicken, the Crab Tart was left in the oven a fraction too long and looked too burnt on the surface to serve. I was in total despair – and so were our two waitresses. They had taken order after order and it seemed as though I had no food ready to serve. To make matters worse, it seemed that everyone wanted the Crab Tart.

For want of space, I had abandoned the tart outside the kitchen door on the picnic table and declared it would have to be off the menu. Catriona fetched it back inside saying something like: "There's nothing wrong with this and I'm going to

menu

First Course

Fresh-baked, homemade wholemeal bread and butt
is served with most of these dishes as appropr

Homemade Soup of the Day
All our soups are homemade, many to tradition

Brandied Chicken Liver Pate
A delicious homemade blend of chicken livers,
orange juice and ground almonds.

Fresh Skye Prawn Tails
Our prawns are delivered to the door on the
by local fishermen. Jumbo prawns, or Norwe
are a Skye speciality. We serve them in th
homemade lemon mayonnaise.

Peat-Smoked Salmon
This superb Hebridean delicacy is peat-smo
perfection on the Isle of North Uist.

Grapefruit and Orange Refresher
For a light, refreshing start to your mea
fresh fruit cocktail.

Mushrooms in Garlic Butter
Button mushrooms in a creamy garlic sauc

Hot Crab Tart
Homemade tart with a delicious, creamy c

three chimneys restaurant

menu

Main Course

Fish

Trout in Green
Succulent Highland rainbow trout, gently poached in white
wine, served sprinkled with finely chopped fresh herbs.

Queenie Scallop Brochettes
With Herby Brown Rice
Skewers of locally caught queenie scallops and scampi tails
in bacon rolls, mushrooms and green peppers, brushed with
melted butter and lemon juice, lightly grilled and served
with brown rice mixed with chopped fresh herbs.

Prawn and Haddie Pancakes
Wholemeal pancakes filled with a creamy smoked haddock and
prawn mixture and topped with cheese.

Vegetarian Pancakes
Wholemeal pancakes filled with celery, apple, mushroom, onio
green pepper and walnuts, topped with cheese and chopped
nuts.

Also, Fish Dish in Season

A choice of potatoes and a fresh, mixed salad bowl, is
included in the price of your main dish. Dishes served with
rice, will not include potatoes.

three chimneys restaurant

menu

Main Course

Meat

Three Chimneys Special Steak Pie
Scottish beef braised in fresh orange juice, makes the
filling for your own individual steak pie, topped with
shortcrust pastry and served piping hot from the oven.
6.50

Grilled Sirloin Steak
A hot grill seals in all the flavour of prime Scottish beef.
Choose from:-
Simply Steak - garnished and served with our homemade mustard
which is flavoured with whisky and honey.
7.75
Chieftain's Steak - garnished and served with melting slices
of creamy Caboc, the chieftain's cheese.
8.25

Heather Honey Chicken
Breast of chicken coated and served in a sauce made with
Highland heather honey, fresh lemon juice and thyme,
garnished with flaked almonds - a delicious combination
of natural flavours.
4.95

Meadowsweet Lamb Hotpot
Meadowsweet wine, with homemade apple and mint jelly are
perfect partners with sweet leg of lamb, slowcooked with
button onions and mushrooms. Meadowsweet wine is made by
Moniack Castle, the Highland winery, from the Meadowsweet
flowers which grow on Skye.
4.75

A choice of potatoes and a fresh, mixed salad bowl, is
included in the price of your main dish.

three chimneys restaurant

serve it. We must get some food out."

Thank goodness she did!

I muddled through the night. I will never know how – through sheer terror, perhaps. One customer sent his son's steak back no less than three times. Thankfully, there were some people there on our first night who have remained regular customers to this day. To them I will be eternally grateful for keeping faith.

The Crab Tart has remained a popular choice for lunch and dinner ever since. On our second night we served 34 covers, which included a party of 10. I was still on my own in the kitchen. As any chef will appreciate, it was immensely difficult, but I was slightly better prepared. On Sunday we had 27. By Monday I had begun to grasp the concept of 'mise en place' and was making headway. Easter weekend is hectic every year – we just learned the hard way.

We did not open for lunch as well as dinner until the first Wednesday of our opening week. That morning I received a phone call from someone who wished to reserve a table for lunch. The caller's deep voice seemed familiar. It was Derek Cooper, the well-known writer, journalist and broadcaster. I was terrified! He ordered Neep Bree (our traditional turnip soup) and... Hot Crab Tart. Derek was one of the first people to write and congratulate us on being included on the list of the World's Top 50 restaurants. He was also one of the first people to write about us in Scotland on Sunday and a few years later, when we began to win awards, he included us in his television series, Scotland's Larder.

Molly,

mum

and the

rhubarb

man

MY MUM had a friend called Molly. She was a near neighbour of ours and, as a small child, I thought she was marvellous. Apart from being the fastest knitter I had ever set eyes upon, she was a real Glasgow girl. Full of fun and laughter, she always dressed with style, looked great with her slightly outrageous (for the 1950s) blonde perm, bold earrings and (shocking!) she wore an ankle chain. Molly also had a perfect house, with an immaculate kitchen, with everything in its shiny, Formica place. I adored any excuse to call in, because there were always treats in store. Don't tell my dentist, but these were goodies such as brown paper pokes full of fudgy brown sugar, jelly cubes or sugar lumps.

Molly also had a Dad, old Mr Brown. And Mr Brown was the Rhubarb Man.

The Rhubarb Man had an allotment at the end of our street where he grew all sorts of good things and had a fantastic shed full of treasures. My brother and I used to sit on the garden wall and wait for him. He would cycle slowly past on his big black bicycle, his trouser turn-ups tucked neatly around his ankles with his cycle clips. He had fixed a wooden box to the back of his bike to carry things in – including rhubarb en route to Molly's kitchen.

At the sound of our greetings, The Rhubarb Man would slowly

dismount from his bicycle and then offer each of us a juicy, sour stick of the cheek-sucking, eye-watering, lip-puckering, pinky-green, chewy, sometimes stringy – delight!

Rhubarb! Rhubarb! How many of us have childhood memories of sitting on the doorstep with a saucer of sugar and a stick for dipping in it?

The shocking pink, softer variety that we see in the shops from quite early in the year is, I fear, a more watery relative of the real, unforced Scottish thing. The strong green stalks, with their russet tinge, keep their shape plus a bit of a bite, even when cooked. I think this is better and the colour is more real. Fresh orange and ginger are perfect accompaniments for flavour. This could be in jam, or a

fruit fool, a sorbet, a crumble or a pie. A compôte of lightly 'stewed' rhubarb served in its own juice with custard, cream, or ice cream, is quite delicious and simplicity itself. Rhubarb makes great chutney too and is excellent in savoury sauces, particularly with lamb or with scallops.

I've tried them all at some stage or another, but the following recipe for Rhubarb and Stem Ginger Parfait with Ruby Orange Syrup has been a great hit in the restaurant. The colour of the juice of blood oranges makes lovely syrup with the pastel pink parfait. Skye rhubarb is usually available from May onwards, but the good thing about it appearing a little later than elsewhere is that I can keep rhubarb on the menu for longer.

Blood oranges are harder to get hold of, and trips to Inverness, Glasgow or Edinburgh are never complete without a massive supermarket shop before the long drive home. Securing delivery of some of the more unusual fruit and vegetables has been a constant problem for me as a Skye chef. Blood oranges, for example, have to be purchased by the whole case at Glasgow market for onward delivery. Items such as these must be ordered in advance via the local fruit and vegetable wholesaler. I never know what the quality of the goods will be like until they arrive here. Sometimes it is preferable to handpick supplies in smaller quantities from the supermarket.

It is symbolic of our time that the

widest selection of fresh fruit and vegetables is available only from the major supermarket chains. Their well-stocked shelves often carry fresher produce than the main markets. Although our delivery problems have improved dramatically in recent years and we have so many more local suppliers growing fresh produce for the restaurant now, I sometimes have to resort to large trolley loads of shopping from the supermarket, especially in winter. I try not to appear embarrassed when the checkout girl asks me what I do with it all!

Rhubarb is one ingredient I look forward to using with enthusiasm. And Molly, if you or yours are reading this chapter, these recipes are for you – and my Mum, the Edinburgh girl.

Rhubarb and Stem Ginger Parfait with Ruby Orange Syrup

STAGE1. COOK THE RHUBARB.

INGREDIENTS:

750g rhubarb, washed, trimmed top and bottom and cut into diagonal chunks approximately 4cm in length.

200g soft light brown sugar.

Finely grated rind of 1 small blood orange.

Juice of 2 small blood oranges.

2 thin slices off a piece of root ginger.

METHOD:

Lay the pieces of rhubarb in a single layer in a shallow, ovenproof dish. **Hide** the pieces of root ginger in the rhubarb. **Pour** over the orange juice. **Sprinkle** the sugar mixed with the orange rind over the top and mix through roughly. **Cover** the dish with a layer of greaseproof paper. **Make** a tight-fitting lid of foil to cover the dish. **Place** dish in the centre of a moderate oven and bake slowly for approximately 30 minutes, until the rhubarb is soft, but still retains its shape. **Remove** from oven and lift out two thirds of the rhubarb with a slotted spoon and place in liquidiser or food processor. **Take** care not to put the pieces of root ginger in the liquidiser. **Liquidise** the rhubarb and set aside to cool completely.

Retain the remaining rhubarb and juices to serve chilled with the parfait. **Remove** ginger before serving. **(Rhubarb** cooked and chilled in this way also can be served as a fruit compôte with cream, ice cream, or custard. **We** serve this in the restaurant with our stem ginger ice cream)

STAGE 2. MAKE THE PARFAIT.

INGREDIENTS:

150ml water.

125g granulated sugar.

3 eggs.

150ml double cream.

I heaped tbsp crystallised ginger pieces, chopped small.

Line a 2lb loaf tin with clingfilm, making sure the clingfilm overlaps the rim of the tin generously, and set aside. **Put** the water and sugar into a saucepan. **Stir** over a low heat until all the sugar is dissolved, then bring to the boil and bubble fiercely for 3 minutes to make a sugar syrup. **Fit** a heat-resistant pudding basin (such as Pyrex) over a pan of simmering water, making sure that it fits snugly and that the bottom of the bowl is not touching the water. **Whisk** the eggs in this bowl (use a hand-held electric whisk if you have one) until frothy. **Pour** on the sugar syrup. **This** must be done with care. **Do** not let the hot syrup touch the whisk. **Continue** to whisk the egg and syrup mixture over the simmering water until the mixture is pale and mousse-like. **The** whisk will leave a ribbon trail in the mixture when lifted out.

Next, lift the basin off the pan of water (take care that the hot steam does not burn your wrist) and whisk until cooled down. **This** can be done while standing the bowl in a basin of iced water, to speed things up. **Whip** the double cream until just holding its shape, but not solid. **Fold** the cream and the rhubarb purée together and add the chopped crystallised ginger. **Fold** this mixture into the egg mixture. **Do** not overstir or you will knock out all the air. **Pour** the finished mixture into the lined loaf tin. **Freeze**.

SERVE THE PARFAIT.

Unmould the frozen parfait on to a flat serving dish. **Peel** off the clingfilm. **Using** a knife dipped in hot water, slice the parfait and place on individual plates. **Spoon** the chilled rhubarb on the side and pour the orange syrup around. **Decorate** as you please. **We** like to use a little piece of very dark chocolate, such as wafer-thin curls. **There** will be enough parfait for at least 8 people. **What** you do not use can be wrapped and kept frozen for another occasion. **You** can easily cook extra rhubarb as an accompaniment any time.

Rhubarb Crumble Tart

This is a slightly more sophisticated variation on the theme of traditional Rhubarb Crumble. I always use rolled oats, chopped nuts and brown sugar in my crumble topping for flavour and texture. In our early years, apple crumble and rhubarb crumble were frequently on the pudding menu.

STAGE 1.

Line a 20cm loose-bottomed flan tin with sweet shortcrust pastry and bake blind in a moderate oven. (Gas Mark 5, 190°C, 375°F)

STAGE 2. COOK THE RHUBARB.

INGREDIENTS:

500g rhubarb cut into diagonal chunks approximately 4cm in length.

Juice of 1 small orange.

2 slices of root ginger.

200g soft light brown sugar.

Follow the instructions for cooking the rhubarb as for the Parfait recipe.

STAGE 3. MAKE THE CRUMBLE TOPPING.

INGREDIENTS:

125g wholemeal flour.

125g butter chilled from the fridge and cut into small pieces.

125g soft light brown sugar.

100g jumbo oats.

100g nibbed almonds, or chopped nuts of your choice.

Half a level tsp of ground ginger.

Rub the butter into the flour until it resembles fine breadcrumbs. Add all the other ingredients and mix well. Keep the mixture loose and crumbly. Work with the butter while it is still quite cold.

STAGE 4. ASSEMBLE AND BAKE THE TART.

Place one third of the crumble mixture in the base of the baked flan case. Place the cooked rhubarb on top in an even layer, filling the flan case. Finish with an even layer of all the remaining crumble mixture. Return to bake in the centre of a moderate oven for 20–25 minutes until golden. Serve the tart warm with fresh whipped cream, ice cream, custard or crème fraîche.

WE ARE often asked how we cope living so far away from a decent shopping centre. Our nearest Marks and Spencer is in Inverness, a 6 hour round trip by car from The Three Chimneys. Some visitors find this hard to imagine.

When we first arrived in Skye, access to the island was still by ferry from the mainland at Kyle of Lochalsh. It was only a short, 5 minute crossing, which made it all the more frustrating if we just missed it by seconds and had to wait 30 – 45 minutes to complete the trip on the next one available. Everyone has stories of 'racing' to catch the last ferry at night, or early on a Sunday evening. Many tales are told of nights spent in the car on the slipway.

In my opinion, the Skye Bridge was long overdue. Critics argued that Skye would lose its island identity and the romance of sailing over the sea to Skye would be lost, to the detriment of the whole community. I believe the opposite is true. The bridge arches dramatically over the sea from the mainland and the mountains beckon everyone to 'come and see'.

Daily life on the island has been enhanced by the advent of the bridge. Improved communications have enriched the local economy, and in general, have made life easier all-round. Few people regret having the bridge, but most people resent the high tolls that were imposed and regard them as grossly unfair. The tolls – paid in both directions – make the Skye Bridge by far the most expensive mile in the whole of the UK trunk road system. Local people can buy a book of tickets that represent a big saving over the cost of a single crossing, but it remains relatively expensive.

During the winter months, there is no other means of getting off the island by car. If one considers, for example, that the region's main general hospital is in Inverness and that most of the island's babies are born there, this may help to put the ludicrous tolls into perspective.

However, very few people living in Skye would choose to do without the bridge now. Those of us running small businesses know only too well how much easier it is to get goods delivered quickly compared with years gone by.

When we bought The Three Chimneys and moved to Colbost from the centre of Croydon, we had the whole winter ahead of us. The plan was to have plenty of time to settle the children into their new home and school and to give ourselves a few months to restyle the restaurant in our own way, find staff, get to know the island and source suppliers. We were starting from scratch with absolutely no local knowledge.

Deliveries were difficult over the first few years. Many big companies refused to deliver any closer than Portree or Dunvegan. We soon realised that the four-and-a-half mile stretch of single-track road to The Three Chimneys from the village was an enormous handicap.

When we first started in business, fresh milk arrived in Dunvegan at 4.30 in the afternoon in the boot of the school bus. Usually, this had sat

on the pavement outside the bus garage in Portree all day, in all weathers. When I complained to the dairy company I was told that there was no call for fresh milk in Glendale and that everyone 'over there' bought UHT! I battled with UHT milk and, worse still, UHT cream for months, but fought to get fresh milk delivered to the north-west corner of the island for quite some time. Having it delivered to the door in the morning is a very recent service.

We have a few delivery tales to tell: of fresh fish arriving from Mallaig with the coalman in his yellow oilskins, black with coal dust; of a 'phone call from the ferryman at Kyle to tell us that 20 cases of wine had been left on the slipway for us, as that was the nearest the van driver had been prepared to travel. Anywhere else in the world and the wine would have disappeared long before we could have reached it! There was no other course of action but for Eddie to get in the car after lunch service and fetch it. Before I had established contacts with local fishermen, I frequently drove to Portree late at night after dinner was served, to collect prawns landed there or at Uig.

But shopping trips to the mainland were what I missed the most, as they were very few and far between in the early years. I was completely tied to the kitchen. If I was not there to cook we could not open the restaurant, as there was nobody else to do the job. Once the season started at Easter, it was heads down all the way through until October. Personal shopping came to a complete halt for months. Opportunities to take the children to have their feet measured for new shoes, to get my own hair cut, or to buy something as basic as a birthday card, were virtually non-existent.

Good enough to eat

FOR ME, freedom means kicking off the kitchen clogs and wriggling my bare toes into a pair of sandals. Once upon a lovely day in May, I was driving to Fort William on the mainland for a rare night away. The tumbling mountain burns looked tempting enough for me to stop off at the roadside to dip my bare toes into their cool, green, icy water for five minutes. Having cold feet is bliss!

I bowled along the open road in bright sunshine under wide blue skies. Surrounded by awesome scenery, I was dazzled by the beauty of the lush greens and wild splashes of vivid colours that are the Highlands waking up afresh to summer – colours that look good enough to eat.

We had seen the winter snowdrops, the early wild daffodils, carpets of primroses, star-like celandines, wood anemones and dainty violets. Now it was the turn of brilliant yellow clouds of gorse along the roadsides. The lower hillsides were shrouded in white hazy veils of hawthorn and rowan blossom. I caught glimpses of deep lilac bluebells mixed with unfurling stalks of new bracken and long shiny blades of grass amongst the trees. Soon there would be a patchwork of purple wild thyme, yellow vetch and bell heather on the road verges too.

What a mad riot of colour at ground level and yet, the deep clefts of the Cuillin and Kintail's great Munro ridges were still

glinting with patches of snow. We had been basking in 70° plus temperatures in Skye and Lochalsh throughout most of May, but on that day, I had driven through two freak hailstorms. These blew in from nowhere and disappeared again just as fast. They say Skye is the place to experience all four seasons in one day. And so it was for me, as I stood in my sandals in a phone box in Broadford, making a last minute call back home. The hailstones were bouncing under the gaps between the ground and the glass panels, giving my bare toes an extra bash for freedom.

Only in Skye! We take the rough with the smooth all the time in the islands. Everyday life is full of contrasts, frequently throwing up unexpected problems to solve instantly. The weather is often responsible.

Wind and storms permitting, the weather is also largely responsible for all the delicious fresh produce we can grow in Skye – as well as the wonderful wild flowers, some of which are edible too. Many people imagine we live in the frozen north, where rain pours down continuously and the sun rarely puts his hat on.

Not so! We have a very mild climate, hardly ever have very bad frost, or deep snow, with the best weather occurring in May and June when it is most needed for new growth. The TV weathermen rarely do us justice. The shipping forecast is the one many of us rely upon. It has become as important to me as a chef, as it is to the fishermen and growers. The weather is a serious topic of conversation here!

Believe it or not, the walled gardens of the grand houses of Skye cultivated a wealth of produce in years gone by. Fresh cut flowers were sent to market in Glasgow via the fish train from Mallaig. Wonderful

varieties of apples and pears were grown in well-sheltered orchards.

Brigitte and Kornelius Hagmann of Glendale are two of Skye's fast-growing fraternity of seriously dedicated horticulturists. Call them modern crofters if you like, for they grow everything within the boundaries of their croft in Fasach. Every inch of ground of their few acres is precisely laid out. It has taken them eighteen years of intense work to be where they are today. As members of the Soil Association, everything they grow is purely organic. Using seaweed and natural compost from their constantly replenished and beloved compost heap, they feed their huge range of lettuces, salad leaves, herbs, vegetables,

edible flowers and fruits and tend them all with precision and care. Later in the summer, peas, beans, courgettes, fresh garlic and cherry tomatoes will become available. By late May, I've already had rhubarb and even fresh asparagus. Gooseberries and red, black and white currants will be ripening for picking in June and July.

Kornelius and Brigitte's success lies in their tireless work striving for perfection. But it also lies in their genuine interest in everything good that grows naturally and, above all, tastes wonderful. Their skills with salad leaves and herbs therefore extend to include edible flowers, both wild and wild-cultivated, in their incredible range of produce. Hand-picked and packed within a few hours of delivery to our kitchen door from Glendale, three miles along the road, I relish my kitchen's ability to create beautiful salads using the contents of the Pandora's cool-boxes that arrive several

times a week. Nothing in this world could be a more perfect complement to the fantastic fresh seafood from the sea lochs of Skye and The Minch beyond. This is Skye on a plate – in all its glorious spring colours.

Recipe for Skye on a Plate

Find a well-tended kitchen garden growing lots of good things. **Pick** an interesting variety of salad leaves such as: **Landcress, Greekcress** and **Mustard leaves, Rocket, Mizuna** and **Minas Lettuce. Add** all sizes and shapes and colours of **Sorrel, Kale** and **Beetroot leaves. Peashoots** are great too. **Add** a few wild ingredients from round about, such as young **Ground Elder, Chickweed** and **Wild Garlic. Select** this carefully and wash it well. **Add** fresh herbs such as **Chervil, Fennel, Lovage, Lemon Balm, Basil, Dill, Tarragon** and **Mint,** to complement the food that you have chosen to accompany the salad. **Mix** the green ingredients together. **Add** a handful of brightly coloured edible wild flowers such as: **Primroses, Celandines, Wild Violets, Wild Pansies, Wild Garlic flowers,** flowers from the **Gorse bush,** plus those from the herbs and leaves used in the salad, such as **Chive flowers, Meadow Parsley, Borage, Fennel, Mustard** and **Kale. Marigold petals** and **Nasturtiums** add a wonderful splash of gold. **Dress** the salad with vinaigrette dressing of your choice to complement the other ingredients. **I** use Lemon and Olive Oil for Lobster and Langoustines, or Orange, Honey and Grainy Mustard for Seared Scallops and Pan-fried Breast of Mallard Duck.

Lemon and Olive Oil Vinaigrette

INGREDIENTS:

2 tbsp freshly squeezed lemon juice.

1 level tsp caster sugar.

1 tsp good quality Dijon mustard.

1 large clove of crushed garlic.

Freshly ground sea salt and black pepper.

150ml virgin olive oil.

METHOD:

Mix all the ingredients together except the olive oil. **Whisk** the olive oil into the lemon base ingredients, slowly, a small amount at a time, until it is well mixed together and beginning to thicken slightly.

Orange, Honey and Grainy Mustard Dressing

INGREDIENTS:

Finely grated rind of half an orange plus 1 tbsp of the juice.

1 tbsp sherry vinegar.

1 tsp coarse grain Dijon mustard.

1 tsp heather honey.

Freshly ground sea salt and black pepper.

10 tbsp hazelnut oil.

METHOD:

Mix all the ingredients together, except the oil. **Whisk** the hazelnut oil into the orange base ingredients slowly, until all is mixed together well and beginning to thicken slightly. **Can** be warmed before drizzling over seared scallops.

Warm Salad of Seared Scallops with Wild Mallard Duck,
Orange, Honey and Grainy Mustard Dressing

This recipe is sufficient for 2 main course meals. You can adapt it for more people, or reduce the number of scallops and the amount of duck to serve as a starter. Prepare your salad ready for serving on each plate before cooking the duck and scallops. Prepare the dressing as in previous recipe. (If you have dressing left over, keep it in a sealed container in the refrigerator and use it at a later date.) Wild mallard is seasonal and only available from September to March. An alternative could be duck or chicken livers lightly cooked and served hot with the scallops, smoked chicken breast sliced cold into the salad, or breast of quail seared in a hot pan as for the duck below.

STAGE 1. PREPARE THE DUCK.

One breast of mallard duck is sufficient per person as a main course. **The** carcass and legs of the bird can be used to make duck stock for soup or game pâté. **Remove** the breasts from each duck. **Keep** the skin on if it is in a good clean condition, if not, remove it.

Season the duck breasts with freshly ground sea salt and black pepper. **Heat** a frying pan until it is very hot. **Add** 1 or 2 tbsp olive oil and heat until it is beginning to 'smoke'. **Place** each breast in hot oil, together with a nugget of unsalted butter, and seal for no more than one and a half minutes on each side. **Remove** and place on a baking tray in the bottom of a hot oven for up to 5 minutes. **Just** before serving, carve each breast into 4 slices. **Keep** warm.

STAGE 2. PREPARE THE SCALLOPS.

Scallops absorb water, so it is important to work with them as dry as possible. **I** prefer to cook scallops whole, but if they are very large, thick and heavy, slice them into 2 discs, through the centre of each scallop. **I** always keep the roe on, although some people prefer to discard this. **Place** the whole or sliced scallops between two sheets of kitchen paper to absorb any surface water. **Just** before cooking, season with freshly ground sea salt and black pepper. **Make** sure your frying pan is very hot. **Pour** in a thin layer of sunflower or olive oil and heat until it is beginning to 'smoke'. **When** the oil is hot, carefully place each scallop into the frying pan and give each one a gentle press flat. **If** you are cutting the scallops in half, place the uncut side in the hot oil first. **Fry** for approximately 30 seconds on each side. **Do** not be tempted to turn the scallops over too soon, or you will not achieve the slightly crisp, caramelised edge around each scallop. **They** take very little time to cook and should be removed immediately from the pan straight to the serving dish.

STAGE 3. TO SERVE.

Arrange the sliced mallard duck and the seared scallops on the dressed salad. **Warm** some of the dressing and drizzle this over the finished dish. **Scatter** with toasted pine nuts or hazelnuts. **Serve** immediately.

MY JOURNEY to Fort William on that beautiful afternoon in late May, was for a special celebration. It was Steven's 21st birthday and we had made an opportunity for a family get-together at Inverlochy Castle Hotel. Steven and Eddie had gone ahead of me to attend a wine tasting that day, and Lindsay was on her way from Edinburgh by bus.

Eddie and I have spent one or two precious nights away at Inverlochy over the years on a few very special occasions. We love it there – the peace and grandeur of its Victorian architecture and beautiful grounds,

all in the shadow of Ben Nevis. It is so relaxing, I once sank into a deep sleep on the sofa in the grand entrance hall and was left undisturbed for quite a few hours.

If you get the chance, go when the rhododendrons are in full flower, alive with the drone of busy bumble-bees diving deep into the voluptuous pink, lilac and purple blooms. We once spent three days there in mid-November with virtually the whole place to ourselves. We explored Glen Nevis and Glen Etive and drove all the way to Ardnamurchan Point at the most

westerly point of the Scottish mainland. We stood there at the lighthouse in the teeth of a gale and an icy squall, completely exposed to the mercy of the elements. A magic moment on a day off as far away from the pressures of the restaurant as we could be. It was dark before we got back to the warmth of Inverlochy with its roaring fire and deep hot bath. Dinner in the beautiful dining room, with its carved, antique sideboards, is always a grand experience of fine food and impeccable service.

Inverlochy will always have a special place in our hearts. The now-retired

Managing Director, Michael Lenard, and his superb staff, have made us so welcome there. Michael dedicated over 25 years of his life to running Inverlochy with absolute professionalism and skill. To us, he is the Grand Master of Hospitality. We learned a lot from his charm, wit and winning ways. He always gave us so much praise and encouragement. Every time we won an award, he would be the first to send us a letter of congratulations. We have a few in our scrapbook, including the envelope for one of them on which he wrote: "Postcode not necessary – it is famous already".

Michael has made a few trips to The Three Chimneys. He once flew in by helicopter with a party of bluff businessmen. He loves fresh Skye lobster, and on that particular occasion we threw together two huge seafood platters for his party to share between them. It was one of those times when I knew that the customers were well-rehearsed in eating out at very fine restaurants. Having landed, miles from anywhere, at our stone cottage on the seashore, they sat down with an air of cynicism, wondering what on earth

they would be offered to eat. Say no more! I loved astounding them with the quality, wealth and flavour of our fresh food, our special service and unique style. A big wink from Michael as he left the restaurant was the only assurance I needed that the visit had been a success.

Family birthdays are special occasions. By the time this book is published, Lindsay will be 21 and I will be 50. Two big days ahead, and as I write, I've made no plans whatsoever. Typical! I have always been left with no time to plan parties, wrap presents and write cards, but usually manage to conjure up a few surprises.

During that notorious year of our first opening, I actually threw a sixth birthday party during Whitsun week for Steven. Somehow this was squeezed in between serving lunch and being ready for dinner during one of the busiest weeks of the year. Don't ask me how I managed, but I have the photographs to prove it! The whole of Primary 1 and 2 from our wee school at Borrodale came for tea and games in the garden. Both the children spent their earlier years at the local primary school before

graduating to Portree High School and a 25-mile bus ride every morning.

Memories of baking and icing cakes in secret, long after midnight, are still fresh in my mind. But like any mum, I would not have missed out on doing so for the world.

Soft
fruits and
thrupenny
cones

THERE HAVE always been Italians in my life, my first loves being the Italian ice cream cafés in Peebles High Street and Morningside Road in Edinburgh. Before the days of home freezers, a large, half-crown tub of 'proper' ice cream from the local café was one of the best of all childhood treats. Being sent to collect it was half the fun. I would rush home clutching my tub of icy white gold wrapped in newspaper and help to dish it into the pudding plates quickly, before it melted. Served with the first punnets of fresh Scottish strawberries from the greengrocer, this was one of those taste sensations that made summer very special.

There has been a strong Italian immigrant community resident in Scotland since the early 1900s. Using their inherent love of good food and culinary skills, together with their natural warmth and friendliness, many opened ice cream cafés and fish and chip shops. A host of inland and coastal towns and villages, particularly around Edinburgh and Glasgow, still boast their own Italian café. For a child growing up in Peebles and Edinburgh, no day-trip to the seaside was complete without a thrupenny cone from a favourite ice cream stop en route.

Perhaps Scotland is more famous for its annual crop of soft fruits than it is for its surprising connection with Italian ice cream. Strawberries must be the most

irresistible of all the summer berries. Soft, luscious and alluring, these plump, heart-shaped berries just beg to be eaten. But raspberries are my all-time favourite. Nothing beats the explosion of ripe flavour that bursts from every berry on the tongue.

It must be at least sixteen years since I was first presented with an overflowing ashet of juicy, freshly plucked fruits from a Glendale garden, in north-west Skye. I was amazed, but delighted, to take them into my kitchen and, later, to serve them to disbelieving customers. The late, but very dear Frank Fawkes would hand over his garden bounty with such pride. He knew how much it was appreciated. Both Frank and his wife Mina would devote hours to tending and picking their crop. Rain or shine, midges, or no midges, they

always fulfilled their promise to deliver in time for lunch. They grew gooseberries, blackcurrants and wonderful lettuces too. Frank's glorious clusters of pink and lilac sweet peas perfumed the restaurant from May to September for many years.

I think of Frank and Mina as being pioneers in the horticulture movement that has since put down such strong roots in Skye. They were the first people to encourage me to use their fresh, local produce in the restaurant and I have never looked back. Today, some of the growers are in full professional production. The strawberries no longer arrive on a large china plate, but neatly packed in plastic containers.

If you grow your own summer crop of strawberries and raspberries, you are very privileged. I depend upon those who produce the most fabulous berries, aided by the island's ideal climate. Visitors to

Skye never fail to be amazed at the quality of the soft fruits grown here.

Running a restaurant is all about creating memorable meals on unforgettable occasions. Finding The Three Chimneys on a summer's evening, with the loch shimmering in the setting sunlight, must be etched on many peoples' memories. The view from the front door must be in a countless number of photograph albums around the world.

As visitors venture indoors, they are frequently surprised to find such a hive of activity so far from anywhere. I believe it is very important that their meal reflects

our unique location, offering a true taste of Skye and all it has to offer in the way of local ingredients. Every course should be as memorable as the one that was served before it. And nothing could be more memorable for dessert than Skye's summer strawberries and raspberries. Eating them with the simplest accompaniment is best – double cream, natural yoghurt, home-made ice cream, or one of the recipes included here.

Soft fruits can be used in many ways other than the more obvious desserts, and they have always played an important role in Scottish kitchens, particularly in sauces for wild game. Recipes for jams and sweet or savoury jellies, made from berries both wild and cultivated, are well documented in our culinary history. A Glasgow friend of mine swears that the first strawberries of the crop should be sprinkled with freshly ground black pepper before eating. Sprinkling them with balsamic

vinegar, or steeping them in Marsala wine is where that Italian influence comes in again!

Strawberries and raspberries still grow wild in Scotland and would have been a more prolific, natural resource to serve with home-made creamy desserts in days gone by. Redcurrants grow wild even in this windswept corner of Skye.

Picking blaeberries, the small, purple fruits of a heather-like shrub that grows on Scottish moors and hillsides, is another enduring childhood memory of mine of holidays in the West Highlands. Later in the year, wild brambles (Scottish blackberries) create another natural source of fresh fruit for puddings and pies, jams and jellies.

Whisky and Lemon Syllabub with Skye Strawberries

INGREDIENTS:

250ml fresh double cream.

Finely grated rind and juice of 1 large lemon.

125g caster sugar.

Half a measure, or 1 generous tbsp, of your favourite whisky.

METHOD:

Whisk all the ingredients together until holding just firm.

Spoon on top of fresh strawberries. **Eat** and enjoy! **Serve** with home-made shortbread biscuits.

Cranachan with Fresh Skye Raspberries

Skye's own malt whisky, Talisker, and heather honey in
particular, are an unbeatable combination of flavours,
perfect with raspberries.

INGREDIENTS:

250ml fresh double cream.

1 tbsp thick heather honey.

1 generous tbsp Talisker whisky.

1 heaped tbsp toasted medium oatmeal.

METHOD:

Toast the oatmeal by spreading an even layer on a flat baking
sheet and leaving it in the bottom of a warm oven until it turns
a darker shade of brown. **Leave** to cool and store in an airtight
container until required. **Whisk** the cream together with the
honey and Talisker. **Fold** in the toasted oatmeal. **Pile** on top of
fresh raspberries and serve. **Raspberries** can be combined into
the cream mixture, but I prefer it served in this way, to enjoy the
full burst of flavour from the raspberries.

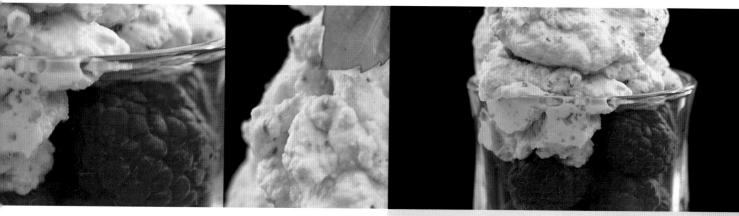

Three Chimneys Shortbread

INGREDIENTS:

375g plain flour.

125g white rice flour.

375g slightly salted Scottish butter.

125g caster sugar.

METHOD:

Cream the butter and sugar together until pale and fluffy.
Work the sifted flour and rice flour into the creamed mixture
until it forms a firm paste. **Knead** it lightly on a well-floured
board. **Roll** it out until quite thin and cut biscuit shapes with
cutter of your choice. **Using** a palette knife, lift the biscuits onto
a well-buttered baking sheet. **Bake** on the centre shelf of a
moderate oven (Gas Mark 5, 190°C, 375°F) until pale golden in
colour. **Remove** from oven and sprinkle liberally with caster
sugar while still warm. **Lift** on to wire tray to cool. **Store** in an
airtight tin.

Summer Fruits Jam

When did you last make home-made jam? Nothing beats the warm, heady summer scent of jam bubbling on the stove – another childhood memory. Like home-made marmalade, there is no shop-bought equivalent. Strawberries have a reputation for not setting easily, but I can recommend making jam with a combination of all the red soft fruits. This will set more easily and tastes excellent. Have a go! White bread from a 'plain' loaf, as found only in Scotland, makes brilliant toast – especially when spread hot with home-made raspberry jam. With a mug of tea and five minutes to enjoy it, this surely must be the height of decadence!

INGREDIENTS:

450g strawberries.

450g raspberries.

450g gooseberries.

225g blackcurrants.

225g redcurrants.

1.8kg granulated sugar.

300ml water.

METHOD:

You do not need to have a specific preserving pan to make jam although it is nice to have one. **A** large, wide saucepan with a thick base will do the job. **Butter** the base of the pan very lightly all over, to help prevent the jam from sticking. **Put** the sugar in a large flat container such as a roasting tin and put it in the bottom of the oven at a low heat, to warm through. **This** helps it to dissolve more easily when you make the jam. **Wash**, top and tail the gooseberries and put them in the pan with the water. **Simmer** gently for about 20 minutes, occasionally crushing the fruit with a wooden spoon. **Wash** and pick over the rest of the fruit and add to the pan. **Bring** this mixture back to simmering point. **Add** the warm sugar, keep the heat low and stir until the sugar is dissolved completely. **Bring** to the boil and keep it boiling rapidly for approximately 10–15 minutes. **Test** that the jam has reached setting point by placing a teaspoonful on a cold saucer. **Push** the jam with your finger and if it wrinkles, it is ready to set. (See page 29.) **Draw** the jam off the heat and skim any white foam off the surface. **Leave** to stand for five minutes, stir once and pot into clean, warm jam jars. **Seal** with jam pot covers while still warm. **Store**, eat and adore.

SCONES AND home-made jam with fresh cream – the ultimate, traditional, Scottish teatime treat.

Desperate to extend the income from our seasonal, stand-alone restaurant, we decided to introduce afternoon tea to the whole day's service. This was in the mid-1990s when the country was still climbing out of

recession and the Bank was on our back constantly, pushing us all the time to be more profitable.

It was so difficult to achieve a high turnover as a seasonal business. Having been closed all winter, we would open at Easter with no more than a handful of bookings in the diary. Apart from the reliably busy

weeks of Whitsun and August, we lived a shaky existence. We were dependent upon tourism and affected directly by the industry's fluctuating market trends.

Things began to improve slowly as we developed our reputation and began to win awards, but Press recognition remained scant and we *had to rely upon our own marketing efforts. Our remote location was an obvious disadvantage and one which we resolved from the very beginning to convert into our unique selling proposition. 'Passing trade' was almost non-existent in the evening. The layout of the restaurant also restricted our customer numbers.*

We inherited several large, Victorian tables when we bought the restaurant. As the years passed and we became a little more sophisticated in style and price, we could no longer expect couples to share these large tables with others. This began to make our numbers even more difficult to attain for dinner. Looking back, it is blatantly obvious why we had to move with the times and make big changes. These included building six beautiful new bedroom suites in The House Over-By and remaining open all year round. Our lives were to change forever.

In the earlier years, afternoon teas were planned to create additional opportunities for passing trade to spend money. Handling the extra workload was a strategic nightmare. To this day, I do not know how we managed to cope.

Me being me, everything had to be perfect. Scones, chocolate cake, coffee cake, shortbread, gingerbread, fruit loaf, home-made jam, lemon curd and whipped cream, were all prepared in our kitchen. The plating-up and tea tray arrangements were quite elaborate, with the dreaded paper lace doilies much in evidence. Eddie developed a complete aversion to paper doilies to the extent that peeling them apart in a (tearing) hurry would enrage him to Basil Fawlty levels.

As an extra burden to our already large workload, we added a selection of freshly cut sandwiches to the afternoon tea menu and decided to offer a few items from the lunch menu until 4.00pm. This meant that the soup was kept going until well after lunchtime, as well as popular items such as hot crab tart.

It was mayhem! As we battled-on with preparation for dinner, we had to leave serving space for snack meals and sandwiches. There were constant interruptions for us to fill tiny ramekins with jam and whipped cream, warm scones, cut cakes – and separate doilies. Customers loved it, but the extra work it created for waiting and kitchen staff hardly balanced. How we kept track of the vast variety and combinations of tea orders that came into the kitchen I will never know. As for the extra washing-up created by the whole event...

Sometimes, I had to help serve and clear the tables because we were so hectic. On one infamous occasion, we served 52 afternoon teas. The

Homebaked Scones £2.00
with cream, or butter, & homemade jam, or honey.

SWEET TREATS

Chocolate Fudge Cake £2.50
with a pot of pouring cream.

Rich Ginger Loaf £1.50
very gingery, served with a pat of butter.

Three Chimneys All-Butter Shortbread £1.00
famous for fourteen years!

Fresh Strawberry Shortcake £1.95
irresitible combination of our shortbread, with fresh strawberries
and double cream.

Selection of Scottish Dairy Ice Creams
served with our Crushed Raspberry, or Dark Chocolate Sauce and
Three Chimneys Shortbread. £2.50 or £1.25 for child's single scoop.

See overleaf for coffee and tea..........

THREE CHIMNEYS RESTAURANT • COLBOST • DUNVEGAN • ISLE OF SKYE IV55 8ZT
Telephone 01470 511258 • Fax 01470 511358

three
chimneys
restaurant

Eddie and Shirley Spear

restaurant filled and emptied twice over, whilst several groups spread themselves outside in the garden. There were toddlers running about, babies on the grass, people looking for toilets. Complete pandemonium prevailed.

If I had not had the support of Ann Knight working with me during those years, I would not have survived. Ann was as close as I got to having a sous chef before Isabel Tomlin arrived in April 1999. She was a maths teacher by profession, but a marvellous cook into the bargain. She had also had the experience of running a bistro operation for a few years.

Ann was the first person I trusted to make bread for the restaurant apart

from myself. Since the early days when my wholemeal bread was the only loaf offered, I had introduced a selection of four varieties. I baked everything myself until 1997 when Ann became a full-time employee and took some of the kneading off my hands. My other notable protégé, Andy McInnes, also learned to bake the bread. He was an instinctive baker, claiming that his Glasgow Granny taught him all he knew. Andy baked the best scones, with a lightness of touch that defied his one-time aspirations to be a professional footballer. He began working at The Three Chimneys as a dishwasher, but stepped into the breach one evening when my only, teenaged assistant caved in under

the pressure, midway through service.

"Dae I jist shoogle these aboot a bit?" were his immortal words as he seized the moment, along with the frying pan handle. Andy's team spirit was paramount at all times – unless of course he had a local league match on, or Glasgow Rangers were on TV!

These foolish things of summer

UNWRAP IT and zap it – a meal in minutes! Today's vast array of shopping choices must surely make life almost effortless for the don't-cooks of this world. It is so easy to buy virtually anything that takes your fancy, ready prepared. But I pity those who regard cooking as a chore and a bore. Taking time to make a meal for yourselves, your family or friends should be enjoyable and not regarded as a slog, or a waste of free time.

Cooking is fun. It lifts your spirits on a bad day. It is a sociable experience. It is done for love and enjoyment. Above all, it is all about giving others a good time.

Which is how I come to gooseberries! Gooseberries are sour, hard, hairy little bullets which make your eyes water and grow on prickly bushes in overgrown areas of the garden.

Why do we bother to pick them? They are pure green gold and taste brilliant – that's why! They are worth every ounce of effort to pick and prepare and can be one of the highlights of a summer meal. But have we forgotten how to enjoy these summertime delights, simply because they involve too much work?

Do you remember the days when you sat on your back doorstep shelling peas on Sunday, de-stalking the blackcurrants, stringing the runner beans, or topping and tailing the goosegogs with an old pair of kitchen scissors?

One of my earliest cooking memories (I was three years old) was visiting

an auntie in summer. She lived in the city and had a big garden absolutely crammed full of excitement. We played 'sardines' in the bushes and rode the battered pedal cars, scooters and trikes endlessly round and round. With my cousins, we were eight children aged from one to twelve. Quite a handful! But we all sat down to eat a meal and we all helped to get it ready – together. I was so proud to be chosen to shell the fresh peas from their pods into the big colander. My older sisters were disparaging of my ability to cope with such an important job, but my heroic Auntie Greta shooed them off!

Auntie Greta is now in her nineties and still going strong in her Bristol garden. She has always cooked. Newly dug potatoes in their jackets turned in melted butter with freshly picked, finely chopped mint, for Sunday lunch; crumbly scones and home-made blackcurrant jam for tea at the end of a long, hot summer's day. Have we all forgotten what a real joy these tastes and experiences were? Remember picking the mint, chopping and mixing it with vinegar to make mint sauce for roast lamb?

If we make just one ounce of effort, we can still save these simple things from becoming buried in the memories of our own time. Keep on cooking. Enjoy the tastes and flavours of real ingredients. Above all, make sure your children have fun finding out what real food is all about.

Gooseberries are gorgeous and they have always grown well in

our Scottish climate. We are one of the few nations that make the most of them as a garden fruit. The old Scots name is groset, one of those Scottish culinary terms that come straight from the Auld Alliance with France. The French word is groseille. Alone, or mixed with other fruits, they make great jam and wonderful chutney. They are perfect when used puréed as a sauce for grilled mackerel – yet

another summertime delight. But they are in a league of their own when used in traditional tarts, pies and crumbles. Ginger is a popular accompaniment for gooseberries, but elderflower is also traditional. The elder blossoms are in flower when the gooseberries are ready for picking. A large head of elderflower, wrapped in muslin and hung in the pot while the gooseberries are cooking, enhances their flavour. I also like to cook them with elderflower cordial, or green ginger wine, instead of a drop of plain water.

If you have never tasted a real gooseberry fool, but have only ever picked up the supermarket variety, you have not lived! Forget the chemical e-numbers, the gelatine and stabilisers. Enjoy making it. Look forward to eating it. Suck

each simple spoonful slowly and indulge. You do not even have to spend time topping and tailing for this recipe. This is a real fool to have fun with!

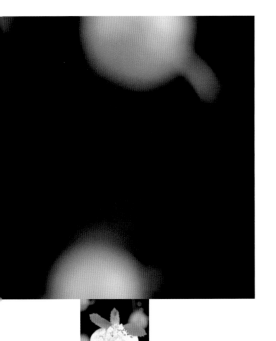

Groset Fool

INGREDIENTS FOR THE FRUIT PURÉE:

500g green garden gooseberries.

1 heaped tbsp caster sugar.

1 tbsp elderflower cordial, or plain water.

METHOD:

Place the ingredients in a saucepan with a well-fitting lid and cook until soft and pulpy, slowly over a low heat. **Liquidise** and pass the purée through a fine sieve. **Cool** completely. **You** can avoid having to top and tail the gooseberries if you are planning to make a purée in this way. **However**, you should top and tail gooseberries going into pies, or crumbles, or in jam or chutney.

TO MAKE THE FOOL:

Whisk 250ml of double cream in a bowl together with 1 tablespoon of elderflower cordial (optional) until thick and floppy. **Fold** in the cold gooseberry purée. **Add** a little extra sugar to taste if necessary. **The** Fool should taste sharp. **Spoon** into a serving dish, or individual glasses, and chill in refrigerator before serving with a shortbread biscuit on the side.

Gooseberry Meringue Tart

Line a 20cm loose-bottomed flan ring, or deep dish, with sweet shortcrust pastry and bake blind. (Gas Mark 5, 190°C, 375°F) **Make** the gooseberry purée as in previous recipe and return to the rinsed saucepan. **Over** a low heat, stir in 50g of butter until melted. **Add** the yolks of 2 large eggs and cook thoroughly, but gently. **Pour** the cooked mixture into the baked flan case. **Whisk** the 2 remaining egg whites until stiff. **Add** 50g of caster sugar and whisk until stiff again. **Fold** in another 50g of caster sugar. **Meringue** should hold in soft peaks. **Spoon** the meringue mixture over the gooseberry purée filling the flan case. **Place** in the centre of a moderate oven (Gas Mark 5, 190°C, 375°F) and bake for 20–30 minutes until meringue is turning crisp and golden. **Serve** the tart either hot or cold, with whipped fresh cream, ice cream or crème fraîche.

ageing and lacking in children of similar age. I researched local information on schools, activities, doctors, dentists and shoe shops, before we made the final decision to buy The Three Chimneys.

I soon discovered that the communities of Dunvegan and Glendale were thriving. Borrodale Primary School, a little over three miles from the restaurant, had a roll of more than thirty children. When Lindsay started school two years later, the roll increased again. She was one of an entrance class of nine pupils – an unusually large intake!

Like all children, Steven and Lindsay were always 'starving' when they arrived home from school, only to find us in the throes of clearing up after lunch and busy with preparation for the next meal.

Leftover jacket potatoes became the family joke, synonymous with 'quick snack'. Occasionally, one of the children would dismiss home life altogether with the disparaging words: "There is never anything to eat in this house!"

Eddie's mother and father, known affectionately to everyone as Nan and Grandad, moved to join us in Skye at the beginning of our third season. They built a house on a patch of ground behind the restaurant and moved in April 1987. In truth, this is how we managed! Nan and Grandad's house became the children's second home. While we were working, Nan cooked their evening meal and made sure they were bathed and tucked up in bed safely each night in our flat above the restaurant. The worst part for me was when Nan sent the children into the kitchen to give me a quick goodnight kiss. As I was usually under stress dealing with the night's orders, it was always a wrench to see them off to bed in such a brief, unmotherly moment.

BEING A mum and a chef are not easy roles to combine, especially if you run your own restaurant and work all day and every night. Every working mum suffers from a guilt complex from time to time, but if you hardly see your children from one Sunday to the next, it is quite hard to shrug it aside. In our early years in Skye, time spent as a normal family was of high value.

Eddie and I had been very conscious that moving the children to a remote island community would not necessarily be a good move if the rural population turned out to be

Meanwhile, as the children slept in their bunks upstairs, the night's business continued, with myself in the kitchen and Eddie waiting front-of-house. The hectic, hot kitchen and the bustling dining rooms were a world away from the serenity of the cosy bedroom above. Not putting the children to bed was the thing I missed the most in those early years. When the last dessert had gone to the table, I would slip upstairs to check all was well.

One of the hardest aspects of running The Three Chimneys was coping during the long summer holidays (one of the busiest times of the year) and the early evenings (one of the busiest times of the day). Encouraging Steven and Lindsay to help with the cooking was all very well, but any job they were asked to do was always 'for the restaurant' and rarely for a family meal. They were brought up in a restaurant where the main kitchen also served as our family kitchen. As they reached their normal teenage years, sharing late Saturday morning breakfast cereal with unsympathetic staff already hard at work was never easy, and something they always hated.

Sometimes, Lindsay would leave a note or a drawing for me on my pillow at night. These were always poignant reminders of the topsy-turvy life we led. Neat little scenes would appear, of a house with a garden, or a living room with a fire and a dog or a cat curled up on a rug in front of an armchair – usually with me in it with a cup of tea. Both the children produced an amazing collection of greetings cards for every occasion, all home-made with drawings in crayon and neat paper cut-outs stuck onto paper. Cartoons of Dad, the stressed-out waiter and Mum, the mucky chef with dirty apron and worn-out trainers, were favourite subject material. I regret not having kept a proper scrapbook of their work. Instead I will find something nostalgic tucked away for safe keeping in a bedroom drawer and wish I could remember when I received it and how old the children were when they drew it.

As they grew older, they played outdoors on their bikes until late. When big events such as the World Cup, Wimbledon, the Olympics or Tour de France were televised, they would re-enact events in the back garden. At least I always knew they were safe!

It was not very long into our new career that we decided to remain closed on Sundays. This gave us invaluable time to spend with the children, as well as a customer-free and staff-free zone for a day. Eddie's Sunday morning fry-ups became the highlight of our family week.

The only downside of those precious Sunday mornings was the public. Even although the 'closed' sign was clearly visible, people would press their noses to the window to look inside, try all the doors and knock to ask if they could use the toilet. One day, Lindsay suggested we should all 'freeze' and pretend to be statues eating bacon and eggs. Much hilarity ensued when we did this the next time we were stared at, particularly as the people concerned continued to stare even harder at the montage before their eyes.

Pearls
of the
deep

A SKYE summer's day comes to life around 4 o'clock in the morning. Seabirds chorus another mother-of-pearl dawn. All is still. The grey heron perches on one leg, statuesque, long beak pointing directly into the seaweed shallows of the loch outside my window.

I am often awake early, although I am not always ready to leap out of bed. But every time I am up in time to catch the dawn, I wish I did so every day. It is the best time to spend alone, collecting thoughts, arranging one's mind. I am a 'list' person and always have a notebook and pencil by my side.

Sometime after 6 o'clock I can watch the fishing boats set out to sea from Dunvegan Pier. If I am still in bed I can hear the reassuring rumble of their engines as they head out across Loch Dunvegan towards The Minch. It is important to me to know that the boats are out, because then I can be sure there will be prawns landed late in the afternoon. If it is bad weather, my day starts with an element of

apprehension, as I hate not having prawns on the dinner menu every night. 'Get prawns' is frequently at the top of one of the pages in my notebook.

Skye seafood is second to none. The local fishermen work from small creel boats. The cold, clear Hebridean seas around Skye are the natural habitat for a variety of crustaceans and molluscs. The waters that wash the island's rocky shoreline with its deep inlets, caves and sheer cliffs, are fished for langoustines (known locally as prawns), lobsters, squat lobsters, brown and velvet crabs. For commercial purposes, mussels and oysters are naturally farmed in the sea lochs. Divers gather scallops from the seabed by hand.

It is a sad fact, but virtually all of these treasures from the sea are sent abroad almost as soon as they are landed in Skye. Packed in ice, or transported live in seawater tanks, they are flown or trucked to the city and continental markets. The prawns in a Spanish paella are infinitely more likely to have been landed on Scotland's west coast than any Mediterranean fishing port. The companies exporting shellfish abroad have created an

easy, ever-ready market for fishermen. Only very small quantities are available for people to buy in shops on the island. Instead, the refrigerated vans are at the pier every evening ready to weigh the catch and drive it all away.

All except the prawns and lobsters I buy, of course! The Three Chimneys is well looked after by Willie Murdo and his crew of the *Sealgair*. Communication used to be late-night telephone calls from myself in the kitchen to the fishermen at home.

"I've had a busy night. I'll need more prawns tomorrow. What's the weather forecast? Will you be going out?"

Today, the fishermen all have mobiles. Usually I can see the boat heading home in the late afternoon at the same time as I receive my call.

"We'll be alongside in ten minutes. How many stone are you wanting?"

A big pot of well-salted water goes on the stove to boil. Within half an hour, two or three stone of lively prawns with their sharp, nippy claws and snappy tails are collected from the pier and delivered to the kitchen door. Within minutes they are cooked, cooled, refrigerated and ready to serve. Nothing could be fresher, or finer. Skye is where these prawns should be eaten, because this is where they belong. They are in peak condition because they have not had to suffer the rough ride to market, storage and handling, before selling to the end-user. Cooking them immediately preserves their tip-top quality. I can guarantee there will still be a spring in their tail when they are served to the table.

I believe it is best to serve fresh prawns, and also lobsters, very simply. Prawns cracked from their pearly pink shells, drizzled with lemon and olive oil vinaigrette and served with some fresh salad, make a delicious meal. I incorporate them into other restaurant dishes too. The shells are saved with

lobster shells to make stock for The Three Chimneys famous Prawn and Lobster Bisque. Because the prawns are already cooked, they need very little more than warming through in a seafood sauce, or to be brushed with melted butter, before flashing under a hot grill.

If you are buying prawns (call them langoustines if you prefer) from your local fishmonger, be sure to check they still have a tight spring in their tails!

Grilled Lobster Vanille

Rick Stein chose this dish when he surprised us with a last-minute booking for dinner on a Monday evening in April 2000. My paperback copy of his book *'English Seafood Cookery'* is extremely well-thumbed in my search for ideas and methods.

INGREDIENTS:

2 firm, lively lobsters approx. half-a-kilo in weight each.

4-6 langoustine (prawn) tails per person, cooked and shelled.

4 heaped tbsp fine white breadcrumbs.

2 tbsp good quality Parmesan.

50g unsalted butter.

A squeeze of lemon juice.

Freshly ground sea salt and white pepper.

4 tsp double cream.

FOR THE VANILLA SAUCE:

1 vanilla pod.

250ml good fish stock.

2 tbsp dry vermouth.

250ml double cream.

125ml milk.

6 egg yolks.

1 tbsp lemon juice.

Freshly ground sea salt (optional).

TO PREPARE THE LOBSTER AND LANGOUSTINES:

Plunge the lobsters into a deep pan of well-salted, fast-boiling water. **The** lobsters should be completely immersed in the boiling water. **Cover** the saucepan immediately with a close-fitting lid. **Retain** a high heat under the saucepan and by the time the water has come back to the boil, the lobsters will be lightly cooked and the colour of their shells will have transformed from dark blue to bright red. **This** will take between 5 and 10 minutes. **Remove** the lobsters from the boiling water and plunge immediately into a bowl of ice-cold water to cool the lobsters down as quickly as possible. **This** arrests the lobsters from cooking further within the heat of their own shells.

When the lobsters are cold, remove the claws and cut each lobster in half, straight down the middle. **Remove** the stomach sac at the head end and the intestinal tract that runs the length of the tail. **Discard** these. **Crack** the claws with a sharp tap from a small hammer or a heavy, blunt instrument such as the end of a rolling pin. **Remove** the claw meat carefully and try to retain the shape of the claws as perfectly as possible. **Remove** the meat from the tail in one whole piece and cut into four chunks. **If** you have a lobster with red roes inside it, or greenish-black tomalley, remove this also and stir into the sauce for added flavour and great colour.

Set aside the meat from each half lobster and add 4 or 6 langoustine tails, removed from their shells, to each portion. **Keep** the lobster shell intact, head and tail still joined together with the legs and long red feelers.

The langoustines (prawns) should be plunged into a pan of salted, boiling water in the same way as the lobster. **They** will cook much more quickly, within 2 to 3 minutes at the most, depending on their size. **Remove** the cooked langoustines from the boiling water and plunge into cold water to cool them down immediately. **Snap** the tail from the head section. **Hold** the tail lengthwise, between both thumbs and forefingers firmly and squeeze the sides of the tail shell together. **You** will hear a gentle crack. **Peel** the shell away from the meat inside and remove the langoustine (prawn) tail intact.

TO MAKE THE VANILLA SAUCE:

Take 1 vanilla pod, cut it in half lengthwise and scrape out the seeds, which will resemble a black paste. **Keep** the seeds on one side and place the pod in a saucepan with 250ml good fish stock, plus 2 tbsp dry vermouth. **Bring** this to the boil and reduce by half to 125ml.

Remove the pod and add 250ml double cream, plus 125ml milk to the saucepan. **Return** to the heat and warm until it is just beginning to bubble around the edges.

Meanwhile, whisk 6 egg yolks together with 1 tbsp lemon juice in a bowl. **Pour** over the warm milk and cream mixture, whisking all the time. **Return** this mixture to the saucepan and heat it slowly until it thickens like a custard. **Stir** all the time and watch it carefully. **When** the sauce is thick enough to coat the back of a wooden spoon, pour it immediately into a clean bowl, jug, or other container and stand it in a bowl of iced water to cool down quickly. **This** will help to prevent the sauce from scrambling as it continues to cook in its own heat. **Stir** in the vanilla seeds.

Check seasoning and add a little salt if necessary, remembering that the addition of all the other ingredients will affect the final flavour of the dish. **Leave** to cool completely. **Sauce** can be stored for later use, in the refrigerator.

TO CONSTRUCT THE FINISHED DISH:

To complete this recipe, you will also need 4 heaped tbsp fine white breadcrumbs, mixed together with 2 tbsp best quality, finely grated Parmesan cheese. **Melt** 50g unsalted butter in a wide saucepan together with a few drops of fresh lemon juice, a twist of sea salt and white pepper. **Put** the prepared lobster and langoustines (prawns) into the pan and gently turn and coat in the butter. (**It** is easier to do this in 2 separate lots than all 4 portions at once.) **Add** 2 tbsp of sauce per portion of lobster meat, together with 1 tsp of cream. **Fold** the lobster and langoustines very carefully together with the sauce and warm through gently.

Place the half lobster shells on 2 separate baking sheets lined with foil. **Pile** the lobster and langoustines, with the sauce, back into the empty lobster shells. **Use** the remaining sauce to cover the meat liberally, filling in all the gaps. **Sprinkle** the top with the breadcrumbs and Parmesan. **Place** one tray of lobster in the bottom of the grill to keep warm, while you prepare the second tray of lobster. **When** all the lobster is ready, place both trays directly under a very hot grill to give the dish a final blast of heat, while browning the breadcrumbs and Parmesan on top. **The** mixture should show signs of sizzling and bubbling up around the edges.

Transfer the whole hot lobster to a warm dish and serve immediately. **In** the restaurant, I serve this dish with a timbale of basmati rice, cooked with some finely chopped onion, lemon rind, cardamom and fresh herbs, together with dressed salad leaves.

Hot Skye Lobster and Langoustines with Brandy and Cream

This is an adaptation of a recipe from one of my Elizabeth David cookery books. When she died in 1992, I decided to include this dish on our menu as my own secret tribute to her memory. I had been planning to include a 'hot' dish of some kind, using prawns and lobsters, and this proved immensely popular. It is important to prepare all the ingredients before you start cooking. Measure out the brandy, sherry and cream and have everything close at hand. Once you start cooking this dish, it all comes together very quickly and there is no time to stop in between each stage!

INGREDIENTS FOR 2 PEOPLE:

1 cooked lobster, approximately 500g in weight.

8 cooked, medium/large langoustines.

(See previous recipe for instructions for cooking live

lobster and langoustines.)

2 small shallots, very finely chopped.

100g mushrooms – fresh chanterelles are delicious in this

dish. (They grow wild in Dunvegan!)

50g butter.

2 tbsp good quality brandy.

2 tbsp good quality dry sherry.

200ml fresh double cream.

1 tsp fresh lemon juice.

A pinch of cayenne pepper.

A few twists of freshly ground sea salt and white pepper.

PREPARE AS FOLLOWS:

Remove the claws and legs from the cooked lobster. **Put** on one side. **Cut** the lobster in half, straight down the middle from head to tail. **Remove** the tail section, whole, keeping the meat intact inside its half shell. **Remove** all traces of the intestinal tract from each half of the tail. **Remove** the stomach sac from the head section and discard. **Scrape** out the soft contents of the head section, particularly if it contains the greenish-black tomalley, as this adds a delicious finishing touch to the sauce. **Remove** the tail meat from the cooked langoustines, as described in previous recipe. **Peel** and finely chop the shallots. **Wash** and pat dry the

mushrooms. **Have** all the other ingredients measured and ready to use.

TO COOK:

Melt the butter in a wide, shallow saucepan that has a thick base. **A** sauté pan is ideal if you have one. **When** the butter is hot and foamy, add the shallots and season with the salt, pepper and cayenne. **When** the shallots have softened, add the lemon juice. **Immediately** place both halves of the lobster tail (shell still on) into the butter. **The** lobster shell should be uppermost and the meat lying in the hot butter. **Allow** to heat through gently for 2 minutes. **Pour** in the brandy and flame it immediately. **When** the flames have died, pour in the dry sherry followed by the cream. **Place** the mushrooms into this mixture once it is beginning to heat up. **Last** of all, add the langoustine (prawn) tails. **When** the cream sauce is reaching boiling point, remove the pan from the heat. **Lift** the lobster, langoustines and mushrooms onto the serving dishes, using a slotted spoon. **Return** the pan to the heat with the cream sauce still in it, and add the soft contents of the lobster head, including the tomalley if available. **The** tomalley will turn the sauce pink. **Stir** well, bring to the boil and reduce until the cream sauce is beginning to thicken. **Pour** the hot sauce over the seafood and mushrooms. **Serve** immediately with fresh salad.

Three Chimneys Prawn and Lobster Bisque

It is only possible to make a good bisque if you have well-flavoured stock for the base. I am lucky to have plenty of spare shells left over from preparing lobsters and langoustines (known as prawns in Skye) in the restaurant. These are frozen until we have enough to make a large batch of stock. It is possible to buy lobster stock from specialist food outlets, such as a good delicatessen, but this may take some investigation for each reader locally. Below is my method.

TO MAKE THE BISQUE STOCK:

You will need the heads, tail and claw shells of at least 2 cooked lobsters and 12 langoustines (I suggest you remove, eat and enjoy the meat from 1 of the lobsters, but save the shell, and remove the meat from the second lobster to add to the finished bisque, together with the meat from the langoustines, saving all the shells to make the stock.)

1 large onion roughly sliced.

1 bulb fennel, roughly chopped, including the feathery tops.

A few leaves from a bunch of celery.

2 large sprigs of flat parsley, with stalks, broken up.

Half a lemon, sliced.

2 bay leaves.

1 tsp whole white peppercorns.

2 tbsp brandy.

50g butter.

0.5 litres dry white wine mixed with 1 litre cold water.

METHOD:

Put the shells in a roasting tin and place on the top shelf of a hot oven for at least 20 minutes to 'roast'. **When** they are hot, dry and brittle, remove from oven and break up the shells into much smaller pieces using the end of a rolling pin, or similar blunt object.

Melt the butter in a large saucepan until hot and foamy. **Add** all the vegetables, lemon, herbs and peppercorns. **Soften** in the hot butter, stirring until well coated. **Add** the roasted and broken shells, continuing to stir well, and break the shells down into even smaller pieces as you go. **When** everything is hot, pour in the brandy and 'flame' it quickly. **Stir** well again. **Add** 1 litre of cold water with 0.5 litres of dry white wine. **Bring** to the boil and simmer for 30 minutes. **Strain** first through a large colander and then for a second time, through a fine sieve. **Reserve** liquid to make bisque, or freeze for later use.

TO MAKE THE BISQUE:

The white and pale green of 1 large leek, finely chopped.

1 small, or half a bulb of fennel, finely chopped.

1 medium onion, finely chopped.

2 small/medium carrots, finely chopped.

1 stick of celery plus leaves, finely chopped.

50g unsalted butter.

1 litre lobster stock.

25g long grain white rice.

4 level tbsp good quality, plain tomato passata.

Juice of half a lemon.

Freshly ground sea salt and white pepper.

150ml fresh double cream.

1 tbsp freshly chopped parsley.

The meat from a small cooked lobster and 12 cooked langoustines, chopped into small pieces.

METHOD:

Melt the butter in a large saucepan. **Add** all the prepared vegetables and stir well. **Cover** with lid, leave on a low heat and cook gently until soft. **Rinse** the rice with cold running water through a fine sieve. **Add** rice to the softened vegetables and stir. **Add** the tomato passata. **Season** lightly with salt and white pepper. **Add** the stock, bring to the boil and simmer for no more than 20 minutes. **Liquidise** the bisque mixture in a blender. **Return** to saucepan and add double cream. **Add** lemon juice, plus salt and pepper to taste. **Heat** the soup and add the lobster, langoustines and chopped parsley just before serving.

I FEEL sure that I must have boiled and peeled more Skye prawns than any other woman in the world. But when we first moved to Skye, I had never set eyes upon anything like the size of the langoustines (known as prawns locally) that are landed here. I did not have a clue what to do with them.

Eddie and I were an item of great curiosity amongst the local population when we first took over The Chimneys. Whenever we met with others at a social gathering or a school event, people would quiz us about our plans. We had been invited to our first party in Dunvegan. Someone I had never met before asked, very directly, if we would be having Skye prawns on the menu when we opened.

Not wishing to offend anyone at this early stage, I replied enthusiastically that I would, of course! She then announced that her man was a fisherman and that she would send him round with some for me to practice recipes with. I learned later that the woman was called Joanie and her husband was Tim Wear. He and his fishing partner, Donnie Warrack, duly arrived at the back door of the restaurant one dark, winter's night, with a carrier bag full of twitching, flapping sea creatures. They looked positively prehistoric. I was appalled. Here was something else I would have to learn to deal with. Bravely, trying not to show my alarm, I picked one up. Scores of black, shiny, bulbous eyes followed my every movement.

"What's the best way to cook these?" I tentatively asked Tim.

"Just boil them as they are in some salted water for two or three minutes," he replied nonchalantly.

And then he proceeded to demonstrate how to crack open a prawn's hard outer shell, using fingers and thumbs.

When Tim and Donnie left, I 'phoned Eddie to tell him about my latest culinary encounter. He was on a training course in Nairn run by the Hotel and Catering Industry Training Board for novices wishing to start up their own business. The whole course turned out to be a valuable introduction to the mechanics of running a restaurant. I had seen the course advertised and had telephoned to investigate. I spoke to a warm, friendly woman call Jess Thomson, who was the very first person to give us real encouragement for our project; the first person to make us feel we were not complete fools and that really, we could 'have a go'. We keep in

touch to this day. She has been like an invisible guardian angel to me.

Once I had mastered boiling the prawns, I began to wonder how I should serve them. They looked spectacular. Could I be bold enough to present them just as they were? Whole Skye prawns, in their shells, with seafood dip, salad and home-baked wholemeal bread? At the time, I had also applied to join the Taste of Scotland scheme, itself in its infancy. The information supplied to us included the name of the new organisation's official Food Adviser, Catherine Brown, now well known as an author and food writer. I took the plunge and 'phoned her to ask if it would be acceptable to the general public if I served my beautiful Skye prawns in this way. She was ecstatic in her enthusiasm for the whole idea.

"Just do it!" she told me positively. "If only more people would do the same!"

I have never looked back. Skye prawns have become a signature dish of The Three Chimneys and the crowning glory on our famous Seafood Platter. They always cause a stir when presented on the plate.

We use at least 60kg of live prawns every week between April and October, serving them for lunch and dinner in a variety of ways. They are on the menu every day, all year round, unless severe weather has curtailed fishing and we have, literally, run out of supplies. I go to great lengths to ensure this does not happen, sometimes making a journey late in the evening, after all the meals are served, to collect that night's landing. There have been many, many occasions over the years when I have been boiling prawns and lobsters long after midnight, listening to the shipping forecast and the strains of 'Sailing By'.

The

glorious

grouse

EVERYONE involved in the great hospitality industry knows only too well that our friends from across The Pond ask frequent questions.

"What is a crofter?" "Are all the sheep free-range?" "Do you grind your own oats?" "Do you churn your own butter?" "Can I have the fruit fool without the cream?" "What is a gooseberry?"

Keeping a straight face is not always easy, especially if you are a waitress with a wicked, Glasgow sense of humour. Barbara Ronald worked with us as our waitress for many years. She was a bundle of Glasgow laughs, as well as being highly professional, a wonderful friend and close colleague. Wood pigeon was on the menu one day, and in a way that only an American could, a customer asked

Babs: "Do you shoot your own?"

"No," she replied, remaining deadly serious and speaking in hushed tones. "We buy our game from a Highland dealer, but we always make sure that all the pigeons are Gaelic speakers."

We do not shoot our own grouse either. Chance would be a fine thing!

Red grouse is a delicacy, and so intrinsically Scottish I am always delighted to put it on the menu. Alas, like our beautiful wild salmon, grouse have become harder to obtain in recent years. Although the shooting season runs from the

Glorious Twelfth of August to December 10th, it is usually only possible to bag a few for the restaurant over a very short period.

I suspect that many of the birds stay in the hands of private shooting parties, or are exported to other European countries for an even higher price than they fetch here. The wee Scottish red grouse is highly prized all over the world. I have read that all attempts to breed the birds in other countries have failed. The birds do not flourish and seem to pine for the hills of home.

Red grouse is reputed to be responsible for creating the Highland railway system. Traditionally, Westminster goes into recess especially in time for all Parliamentarians to head off to

the Highlands and the joys of the shooting butts, untrammelled by the affairs of state. I wonder how many of our MPs and MSPs still head for the Highland heather moors in August?

Grouse needs to hang for a week to ten days, depending upon its age and the weather at the time. This makes a mockery of the annual race among top city hotels and restaurants to be the first to serve grouse on the Glorious Twelfth. It is not ready for eating on the day it is shot.

I can remember watching a black and white newsreel at the cinema. Grouse were being raced by train from Inverness to the Savoy in the Strand. The names and pictures of London conjured up such excitement, I longed to go there and see it all for myself. However, I am a complete convert now – an advocate for cooking and serving our wonderful fresh Scottish produce here in Scotland, where it truly belongs, on our own tables, great and small.

Grouse is regarded as the finest game bird of all. Being almost entirely heather-fed, it has a full, but very distinctive flavour that is softer and more delicate than other game. The meat is paler than pigeon or wild duck, for example, and is more velvety in texture. It is the best of all game birds and I love it! Young birds should be roasted in a hot oven quickly (about 10 minutes at most) and left to rest in a warm place. The older birds are used traditionally, in slow-cooked stews, soups and pâtés, for which there are recipes recorded in the annals of Scottish cooking over the past few hundred years. Writers and diarists have waxed lyrical about the aroma of such dishes cooking upon the stoves of Scotland for generations.

I sear the breasts in hot oil and butter and then leave them to rest in the bottom of the oven before serving. I use the carcasses, chopped smaller, to make the stock for the sauce. When it is roasted whole, you must guard against it becoming too dry. A

knob of butter mixed with some fresh berries, or lemon juice, and salt and pepper can be placed in the cavity of the bird. Sprigs of heather soaked in whisky can be laid across the breast of each bird with rashers of bacon. The use of berries in season, such as wild raspberries, blaeberries and rowans, is recorded in many old recipes. With this in mind, I devised a sauce using local blackcurrants (for a sharp fruity taste) and beetroot (excellent together with blackcurrant, for an earthier flavour). I use a tiny amount of bitter chocolate for depth and richness. If you are fortunate to be able to collect wild brambles or blaeberries, replace the blackcurrants with these for an even more authentic taste of Scotland.

Other traditional accompaniments for roast grouse include crispy game chips, a bundle of fresh watercress, skirlie and a spoonful of game jelly, such as rowan or hawthorn. I love using white turnips at this time of year, delicious mashed or creamed with a little grated nutmeg. One of my local growers, Malcolm Golding, produces baby carrots and turnips with the most amazing flavour.

Roast Crown of Red Grouse with Beetroot and Blackcurrant Game Gravy

You will need 4 young grouse for 4 people. You can buy them oven-ready from the butcher in season, but some
readers will have access to their own supply. Either way, you must wash the birds inside and out and scrape away the
remains of any feathers. Check for obvious shot. Carefully remove the legs and the base of the carcass from each bird,
leaving the 'crown' intact (i.e. both breasts attached to the bone). The legs are used to make the sauce.
Discard the base bone, which can impart a bitter taste to stocks and sauces.

TO MAKE THE SAUCE:

50g unsalted butter, cut into cubes and set aside in the freezer to keep well-chilled.

8 grouse legs.

3 tbsp olive oil.

6 juniper berries.

4 cloves.

4 large sprigs of thyme.

2 bay leaves.

Half a tsp black peppercorns.

1 large onion, chopped small.

4 large dark flat mushrooms, chopped small.

225g beetroot, chopped small.

50g blackcurrants (brambles or blaeberries are alternatives).

1 tbsp thick heather honey.

25g extra bitter dark chocolate, finely grated.

750ml red wine.

250ml port.

1.5 litres pre-prepared game stock, home-made is best.

METHOD:

Heat the olive oil in a large, heavy-based pan. **Sear** the grouse legs in the hot oil until they are well browned all over. **Throw** in the juniper berries, cloves, peppercorns and thyme at the same time. **When** the grouse is brown, add the chopped onion and cook until beginning to soften. **Add** the mushroom, beetroot and brambles. **Stir** everything together well. **Add** the heather honey and stir well. **Everything** should be very hot and sizzling. **Pour** the red wine and port over the mixture and stir well to deglaze the pan. **Bring** the liquid to boiling point and leave it to reduce to a small amount. **This** should have a syrup-like consistency.

Add the grated chocolate and stir until it melts. **Pour** in the game stock, bring to the boil and leave to simmer slowly, until reduced by half (approx. 1 hour). **Strain** the mixture, firstly through a large sieve and then again through a fine sieve or muslin. **Return** to a smaller pan and reheat. **Whisk** the chilled cubes of butter into the hot liquid, one piece at a time, until the sauce begins to thicken a little. **The** butter will make the sauce glossy. **Strain** once again and keep hot until ready to serve. **A** few blackcurrants and finely diced cubes of beetroot can be stirred through the sauce when served.

TO ROAST THE GROUSE:

Young grouse take very little time to cook in a hot oven. **At** the restaurant, we place a sage leaf and 2 strips of streaky bacon over the breast of each bird and secure it with string. **We** heat olive oil with a nugget of butter in a heavy-based frying pan and brown each bird all over before placing it in a warm roasting tray in a hot oven for approximately 10 minutes. **The** birds should be left to rest in a warm place (such as the bottom of the oven, or a hot shelf) for up to 10 minutes, before serving whole, on the bone, with your choice of vegetable accompaniments. **Obviously**, remove the string before serving! **You** can partially carve the bird by slicing the breast through to the bone, but leaving it in place. **The** photograph shows the grouse with potato galette, skirlie, spiced red cabbage, beetroot and blackcurrant game gravy. **Skirlie** is traditional oatmeal and onion stuffing. (See page 21.) **If** you can save the grouse liver, this is usually cooked in a little butter and chopped to a fine paste. **Spread** this on a croûton of fried bread and sit the grouse on it in the roasting tin. **The** croûton would be served with the whole roast grouse instead of the potato galette, and game chips could replace the potato element of the dish.

Potted Grouse with Bramble Jelly

A traditional way of preserving cooked meat and fish was to pot them into small moulds or containers. These were then sealed with a thin layer of clarified butter and would keep well in a cold larder for a number of weeks. Potted meat and fish are an excellent standby for lunch parties and picnics, particularly if you are entertaining a large number of people. They can be made well in advance, potted in small ramekins and, nowadays, frozen until required.

'Old' grouse are used in dishes that require slow cooking and are ideal for this recipe.

INGREDIENTS:

2 oven-ready grouse, washed and patted dry on kitchen paper.

120g streaky bacon, chopped into small pieces.

120g belly pork, chopped into small pieces.

120g chopped onion.

1 clove garlic.

1 bay leaf.

1 large sprig of thyme.

Freshly grated nutmeg.

6 allspice berries.

1 bottle fruity red wine.

1 tbsp brandy.

1 level tbsp bramble jelly.

METHOD:

Melt the butter in a large, heavy-based saucepan. **Soften** the onion in the hot butter. **Add** the bacon and cook until the juices run. **Put** the grouse in the pan and brown it all over. **Add** the chopped belly pork, the crushed garlic, bay leaf, herbs and spices. **Stir** everything together thoroughly. **Pour** in the red wine. **Bring** to boil and simmer until grouse is cooked and the flesh is coming off the bones easily. **Remove** grouse from pan and leave aside to cool. **Strain** the remaining liquid through a large sieve. **Retain** the chopped meats and the onion. **Discard** the bay leaf, thyme and allspice. **Return** the juices to the saucepan and reduce until the equivalent of 6 tablespoonfuls remain. **Stir** in the bramble jelly until melted in the warm juices. **Remove** the meat from both grouse and chop into small pieces. **Return** the cooked meats and the onion to the reduced liquid, together with the grouse meat. **Add** the brandy.

Blend all the ingredients in a food processor until the mixture resembles a smooth pâté. **Pot** the pâté into ramekins and freeze or refrigerate until ready to use. **Check** seasoning. **Decorate** with fresh brambles and a sprig of thyme before serving. **This** pâté is delicious eaten with oatcakes and fresh watercress.

I FIRST took Eddie and his nine-year-old daughter, Sarah, home to Scotland in August 1975. We had known each other for a few months and it was time to introduce them to my parents, Peebles and the Scottish Borders.

Eddie's grandmother was Scottish (a fact that would allow him to play football for Scotland, much to the amusement of the kitchen staff) but he had never been there before. Born and brought up in Croydon, he was my driving instructor when we met.

Having gone through an unsettled period in his life, he had taken the driving instructor's job largely because it came with a free car! His previous career had been with Heal's and Habitat, at first learning the soft furnishings trade, but later, as Habitat's youngest branch manager

of the time, responsible for opening the new Bromley branch.

I was working in the Press Office of South Eastern Gas in Croydon. Aged twenty-two, I edited the region's bi-monthly staff newspaper, a job that took me all over the south of England. I gathered and wrote all the material, arranged photographs, did the page make-up and saw the whole job through to print. This was long before the days of computers. I calculated each page layout with my metal printer's rule and a book of typefaces, cropping and sizing photographs with an overlay, to fit my column inches.

I had originally moved to London as a naïve nineteen-year-old with a vague idea of becoming a journalist. I found an interesting job as an advertising assistant to start with, and on one occasion this took me to a meeting of high-powered account executives at one of London's top agencies. I was invited to join the men for lunch at Lacy's near Tottenham Court Road. To this day, it must be one of the most memorable

restaurant meals of my life. The amazing food, the ambience of the white-vaulted interior, the huge round table with the beautiful platter of vegetables – this was what eating out was all about. I was hooked.

The restaurant was run by Bill Lacy and his wife, the cookery writer, Margaret Costa. Strangely enough, I used many ideas from her book, Four Seasons Cookery Book, to develop The Three Chimneys menu. I did not realise the connection until some years later.

Cooking was purely a hobby in those early London days, but something I had always loved doing since a very young child. When I first met Eddie, a love of good food was one of our mutual interests as a couple. Mostly, I would cook dinner for two at the weekend, on the green Baby Belling in my flat. When we could afford it, we loved eating out. Sometimes we drove up to London's bright lights for an evening at somewhere like Manzi's, a fish restaurant just off Leicester Square. Another favourite was Le Chef in Connaught Street. This was a traditional French bistro, very basic in its style and decor, but serving delicious, simple food. I adored going there and greatly admired the chef's uncomplicated approach to cooking. I began to imagine I could create a Scottish equivalent.

It was following the August trip home to Scotland that Eddie, Sarah and I found a house together. Life began all over again for the three of us and I got promotion to the Press Office at British Gas Headquarters near Marble Arch. My commuting days had begun.

Part of my new job was to 'look after' the Home Editors of national magazines and newspapers. Anything they wanted to know about gas appliances – I was the contact. One of the best aspects of my job was occasionally 'entertaining' journalists to lunch. In the mid-1970s, the London restaurant scene was a melting pot of traditional and new. Long-established eateries such as Rules in Covent Garden and Simpsons in the

Strand commanded a wide following. Younger journalists preferred the new breed of restaurants that were opening, such as Langan's Brasserie and Carluccio's Neal Street Restaurant.

As a Scot living and working in London, I was often perplexed by Scotland's poor reputation for its food and cooking. I was frequently the butt of jokes about haggis and deep-fried haddock. Granted, good restaurants were few and far between in those days and it could be difficult to find anywhere reasonable to eat in rural areas. But the restaurant culture predominant in London and based upon French haute cuisine simply did not exist in other areas of the UK. By the 1980s changes were beginning to take shape. Regional restaurants were building a reputation and the movement to serve dishes with an emphasis on regional style and local produce was growing.

Scotland's culinary heritage is based upon its wonderful natural larder and simple meals that were cooked

in every home. In the larger kitchens of the grand country houses and shooting lodges, the culinary expertise was created by intuitive female cooks. There was no male hierarchy as found in the city restaurants and hotels of Europe. Old recipes for intrinsically Scottish dishes are well documented. Many are based on the simplest of fare. In any other country, rustic dishes are promoted with pride as traditional cooking. Every country's classic dishes stem from good use of their region's best ingredients. Scotland is no different.

I resolved in my younger years to take pride in my country's rich resource of traditional recipes. The recipe that would eventually create The Three Chimneys was beginning to take shape.

Late summer harvest

THE BIG harvest moon rising over Loch Dunvegan is a sight to behold. Like a great golden dome it shimmers low on the horizon in the balmy evening sky. That all-knowing, beaming face throws a sash of rippling light across the water, almost to our doorstep. Summer is turning into autumn and, at last, we have slipped into serene September.

The very first time Skye cast its spell over me, it was at this magical time of year. That was almost thirty years ago, but some things have never changed. The hills are still purple-clad in heather, the rowans are laden with red berries and September showers will always create colour-sharp rainbows.

However, eating out on the island has been revolutionised over recent years. The supply of quality, local produce has improved beyond measure. The island now creates its own astounding natural harvest and, late in September, Skye and Lochalsh confidently stages its annual Food and Drink

Festival to celebrate this success.

I bought all of the vegetables in the photograph – plus many more – from members of the Skye and Lochalsh Horticultural Development Association, who grow fruit, vegetables, salads and herbs of all varieties on their crofts throughout the whole area. Beetroot, broccoli, kale, cabbages, cauliflowers, courgettes, lettuces, cucumbers, tomatoes, herbs, peas and beans of all kinds, potatoes, carrots, turnips and neeps... the list is endless. There is also no end to the skill and patience of the growers.

One swift look around their weekly stall, set up in Portree throughout the summer months, instantly belies some peoples' preconceived idea that the Highlands and Islands are bereft of fresh vegetables. Thankfully, those days have long gone!

As visitors drive around Skye, dodging maddening sheep grazing unperturbed on the verge of every single-track road, it is hard for them to understand why Skye lamb is not a local speciality on every restaurant's menu.

Skye lamb is lean, tender, close-textured and full of flavour. Roaming free, sheep feed naturally upon both the heather and wild grasses of the hills, and the seaweed on the shores of the sea lochs. Lambing-time is late in Skye, from around mid-April to mid-May. Many of the new lambs are sent to overwinter and fatten on bigger farms on the mainland. They are eventually sold on, some via the abattoir at Dingwall, which serves a large area of the Highlands. Skye no longer has an abattoir, the battle to restore this service to the island being lost in a maelstrom of EC legislation and financial restrictions.

The original Skye Lamb project was aimed at marketing Skye-reared lamb as a premium brand. Skye farmers and crofters were encouraged to keep their

lambs on the island over the winter and fatten them to a good weight themselves. Once they reached a good weight, the lambs were sent to Dingwall for slaughtering, before being returned via a wholesale butcher to the island's hotels and restaurants, where the meat was sold as a top quality product.

Cooking and serving fine Highland lamb is a joy. The few opportunities I have had to sell Skye's own lamb in the restaurant have proved how highly it is rated by all those who taste it.

There is a considerable financial risk associated with overwintering lambs in Skye and there was a definite reluctance among many crofters to commit themselves to the scheme and the extra workload involved. The logistics of butchering

and selling specific cuts back into the restaurant trade proved difficult within a reasonable price structure that suited everyone.

The whole project began with great promise but, very sadly, the main stalwarts eventually lost heart and the scheme floundered. All may not be lost however, because I believe that the whole food production industry is going through a major time of change, just as the regional restaurant trade has done over recent years.

Greater emphasis is now placed upon the importance of selling fresh, local ingredients. A growth in customer demand may mean that local production on something like the scale of the Skye Lamb project will become the norm. Members of the butchery establishment may be the people who find they are forced to move with the times in the long term. They may be forced to change their seasonal pricing practices and review their overall approach to sales and marketing. Skye and

the Highlands have a world-beating, quality product in their heather-fed lamb. A more imaginative approach to selling it at a premium is long overdue. Meanwhile, I will do everything in my power to encourage that customer demand!

In celebration of Skye's September harvest, I have chosen a recipe that combines fresh vegetables and lamb in the most traditional way –

a broth. Hairst Bree (Harvest Broth) is a lighter version of Scotch Broth, using all the freshest (not dried) vegetables available at this time of year, including broad beans and fresh garden peas and thinly shredded kale or cabbage. This soup is also known as Hotch-Potch.

The traditional Scottish vegetable dishes of Rumbledethumps,

Kailkenny and Clapshot are all delicious served as an accompaniment to grilled or roast lamb. The Leek and Mushroom Pearl Barley Risotto combines a number of ingredients traditionally served with lamb, but presented in a more modern style. Wild garlic is a springtime ingredient, but I have given some alternatives for other times of the year.

Grilled Loin of Lamb with Leek and Mushroom Pearl Barley Risotto and Wild Garlic Gravy

You will need one whole half loin of lamb for 4 people. Ask the butcher to strip the loin from the bone and trim it down to the 'eye'. Remove the fat. Keep the bones to make a good lamb stock for the wild garlic gravy, or any other sauce that you decide to serve. The stock can also be used to make the pearl barley risotto.
Marinade the strip loin of lamb for up to 4 hours before cooking.

MAKE THE MARINADE WITH:

8 tbsp olive oil.

2 strips orange peel (no pith).

2 sprigs rosemary.

2 cloves garlic, crushed with the flat blade of a knife.

8 black peppercorns, lightly crushed.

A pinch of coarse sea salt.

TO COOK AND SERVE THE LAMB:

Pour the marinade ingredients over the meat in a suitable flat dish, cover and refrigerate before cooking. **Grill** the whole piece of lamb under a high heat for approximately 3–5 minutes on each side and then leave to rest in a warm place before cutting into 4 portions, slicing and serving. **This** cut of lamb is very tender and only needs to be cooked lightly. **It** should be pink in the middle. **Along** with the pearl barley risotto, we serve the lamb on a bed of spinach, 'wilted' quickly in hot butter with freshly ground black pepper and freshly grated nutmeg. **Immediately** before serving, pour the gravy around the meat.

INGREDIENTS FOR THE PEARL BARLEY:

200g pearl barley, rinsed in cold water through a sieve.

1 medium leek (avoid too much dark green) and

1 medium onion, both chopped finely.

50g plump raisins.

50g pine nuts.

Finely grated rind of half an orange.

1 tsp finely chopped fresh rosemary.

Freshly ground sea salt and black pepper.

500ml lamb, or light vegetable stock.

250ml good quality red wine.

2 tbsp olive oil.

METHOD:

Heat oil in a wide, heavy-based pan. **Add** pearl barley and keep turning it in the hot oil until it starts to colour pale brown. **Add** the chopped leek and onion, and once softened, add the raisins, pine nuts, orange rind, rosemary and seasoning. **Stir** all together well. **Pour** in stock and wine. **Bring** to the boil and simmer uncovered, until all the liquid has been absorbed. **The** pearl barley should be cooked al dente. **This** mixture can be cooled and stored in the refrigerator at this stage.

TO SERVE:

Roughly chop approximately 200g of assorted wild mushrooms, or whatever you can obtain, depending on the time of year. **Melt** 50g of butter in a medium/large sauté pan and turn the mushrooms in the hot butter. **Add** 2 tbsp of the pearl barley mixture per person to the pan. **Stir** together well. **Add** approximately 1 tbsp of cream per serving, stir well until all is heated thoroughly. **Spoon** onto the plate as a bed for the meat, or shape in a vegetable ring mould, as illustrated. **Finally**, pile a few more sautéed mushrooms on top of the risotto.

TO MAKE THE WILD GARLIC GRAVY:

Wild garlic is only available in late spring, therefore this recipe can only be made at the same time of the year. **However**, you can follow the basic principle and flavour the sauce with different herbs, such as rosemary and thyme, and jellies such as rowan or redcurrant and red wine, or port instead of Madeira. Pick the wild garlic leaves as fresh as possible before using. **The** pretty white flowers are edible and can be used to garnish the dish.

INGREDIENTS:

1 medium onion, finely chopped.

125g mushrooms, chopped small. Use up the trimmings, stalks, etc of the mushrooms prepared for the risotto.

1 fat clove of garlic, crushed with the flat blade of a knife.

1 bay leaf.

A large handful of wild garlic leaves, washed and roughly chopped.

Freshly ground sea salt and black pepper.

50g unsalted butter.

125ml Madeira.

500ml well-flavoured lamb stock.

1 level tsp arrowroot.

METHOD:

Melt the butter in a wide, heavy-based pan. **Soften** the onion and garlic in the hot butter. **Add** the mushrooms, plus the wild garlic and all seasonings. **Stir** together well and allow to cook for a minute or two. **Add** the Madeira. **Bring** to the boil and reduce the liquid until it is thick and syrupy. **Add** the lamb stock, bring back to the boil and reduce again by half. **Strain** the liquid through a fine sieve. **Press** all the liquid through. **You** should be left with 250ml for the gravy. **To** finish, dissolve the arrowroot in 1 tbsp of water. **Mix** until smooth. **Add** this to the gravy in a small saucepan and return to the heat. **Bring** to the boil, stirring all the time, until the mixture is very lightly thickened. **Last** of all, throw in another handful of finely chopped wild garlic leaves. **Leave** these to infuse in the sauce for extra flavour. **Reheat** and strain the gravy before serving.

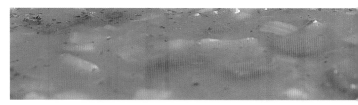

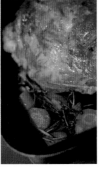

Hairst Bree

Put a neck of lamb in a good-sized soup pot and cover with cold water and a little salt. **Bring** to the boil, gently. **Remove** any scum with a slotted spoon. **Add** 50g of pearl barley, cover the pot with a lid and simmer for at least 1 hour. **Meanwhile**, prepare the harder root vegetables. **Use** the freshest available. **Home-grown** are best, of course! **You** will need approximately:

2 medium-sized, or 6 baby carrots, washed and peeled (or scrubbed), cut into small dice; 1 medium-sized white turnip, peeled and cut into small dice; or, 2 or 3 large slices of neep (swede) peeled and cut into small dice; 2 medium-sized new potatoes, scrubbed and cut into small dice; 1 large onion, chopped small. Vary this selection according to your choice and availability.

Add these vegetables to the meat and barley broth. **Replace** lid and continue simmering on a very low heat for 30 minutes. **Meanwhile**, prepare the finer vegetables. **Again**, use the freshest available, to give full flavour to the finished broth. **You** will need approximately:

The beans from 8 broad bean pods, shelled; 250g of peas shelled from the pod; 4 spring onions, finely chopped; a few small florets of broccoli and cauliflower; a few green beans and/or mange tout, chopped into small chunks; 1 small yellow and 1 small green courgette, cut into small dice; a few fine leaves of curly kale, or approximately a quarter of a fresh savoy cabbage, shredded very finely.

Add these vegetables to the broth, replace the lid and cook for a further 15 minutes. Remove the neck of lamb, cut and serve separately, but with the broth. Or, remove the meat from the bones, cut it into smaller pieces and return it to the broth. The first way is traditional, the second more acceptable today. Check and adjust seasoning. Just before serving, stir in a tablespoonful of finely chopped fresh parsley and mint. This soup stew should be quite thick and makes a meal on its own.

Kailkenny

Prepare enough potatoes, carrots and neeps for the family as usual. Boil in salted water, drain and mash all three together, with butter, salt and pepper. Keep hot.

Shred a head of curly kale very finely. Place it in a saucepan with a knob of butter and cover with a close-fitting lid. Allow it to cook gently over a very low heat. Add no water, the kale will produce enough liquid of its own to cook in. Stir well from time to time until it begins to 'wilt', but retains some of its crispy texture. This will only take a few minutes. Stir the kale into the potato mixture, check seasoning and ensure it is all hot before serving. Savoy cabbage, thinly shredded, can be used instead of curly kale.

Rumbledethumps

Simply cabbage or kale, lightly cooked as before, stirred into mashed potato, seasoned and served hot. Delicious!

Clapshot

Mash together equal quantities of boiled potatoes and neeps with butter. Season with salt, pepper, a pinch of ground ginger and stir in a tablespoonful of chopped chives. Traditionally served with haggis. This must be one of my favourite comfort foods!

I WAS *on a Highland camping holiday the very first time I came to Skye in September 1974. After several damp nights in a tent, struggling to keep the Primus stove alight in the wind, I decided I needed a hot bath and a hairwash. One night of luxury in a Bed and Breakfast was an urgent requirement.*

This was the stage in my life before I met Eddie and I had a very different travelling companion. On that particular day, we made a spur of the moment decision to take the ferry to Skye and followed the road north-west towards Dunvegan, because I had heard about its famous castle.

Having been given vague directions to a B&B in Colbost, by someone who hailed us from his tractor in a field near the roadside, we eventually found Jessie Mary's traditional whitewashed house. It stood back from the single-track road and had magnificent views of Loch Dunvegan, the castle on the far shore and the Cuillin Mountains in the distance.

To my mind, Jessie Mary was the

epitome of the original, Highland B&B lady. We were given a grand welcome, tea and home-baking, a clean, comfortable room and directions to the nearest place for an evening meal. Ten minutes walk along the road and I entered The Three Chimneys Restaurant for the very first time.

The restaurant occupied only one of the rooms of the cottage as we know it today. The kitchen occupied the inner room, just as it would have done since the house had been built at the turn of the 20th century. As we lifted the door latch, we found ourselves in a dimly-lit room, the stone walls cluttered with crofting paraphernalia, and a small stack of peats glowing on the floor of the

flagstone hearth. There were a few communal tables, and as it was not busy, there were plenty of chairs. Dinner was grilled mackerel and chips, washed down with a few beers. This was a feast compared with the previous few nights and we savoured every delicious mouthful. In fact, it was so good we decided to stay at Jessie Mary's for a second night and returned to The Three Chimneys for another meal. The experience was the highlight of our Highland holiday – and never to be forgotten!

In February 1984, almost ten years later, I stumbled upon The Three Chimneys once again. This time it was in a brochure – and it was for sale.

From sheltered gardens

STRONG, SOLID, Scottish stone walls have surrounded generations of everyday life in all forms, since the brochs of early man. From castle keeps and huge estates to cottages and tiny backyards, walls have created homes, provided shelter and built boundaries of all kinds.

One such wall has been lovingly restored in Skye. It surrounds the beautiful old garden of a house that dates back to 1740. The owners have researched its design and creation and believe it to be dated around 1800, or earlier. The garden is unusual, in that it was designed to be more than just a kitchen garden, as most walled gardens were originally. This one grows vegetables on the south-facing slopes, but also has a beautiful pleasure area stocked with scented roses. And at the bottom of this

wonderful walled garden is a very old orchard.

A 250-year-old house overlooking The Minch, with the high hills of Harris on the near horizon, would not normally be associated in one's mind with fruit trees and orchards. The sunny south would seem to be a more likely area of the country, compared with the wild north-west coast. But walled gardens were built for many of the grander old houses, all over Scotland. Their stone boundaries provided warmth as well as shelter and a supporting structure for the plants and trees. Stone soaks up the heat from the sun, as well as

providing protection from the wind and perilous invaders such as rabbits.

The owners of this walled garden in Skye (there are others besides) discovered it in a complete state of neglect and abandonment. Cattle and sheep had been allowed to forage there and indeed, one of the old walls had been bulldozed over purposely, in order to let them in. This move had damaged and destroyed an old quince tree, but very old apple, pear and plum trees survived, and today are bearing fruit. Some of the old trees have fallen, or bent right over with weather and old age, but these are being preserved and used to help regenerate new trees. As part of their mission to restore their walled garden to its original glory, the owners have grafted the old fruit trees to new trees and in this way, are also preserving some of the forgotten varieties of apples and pears.

There is something magical about a walled garden that has fascinated me since I was a small child. I was very young when I fell in love with the story of *The Secret Garden*. I adored the intrigue of the hidden door in the wall, the finding of the old key, the secrets of the overgrown interior. The first time I visited my Grandmother I was only three years old, but I remember being in awe of the secret entrance to her home.

A huge stone wall ran the length of the road. We stood on the narrow pavement in front of a large wooden door in the wall and rang the doorbell beside it. There was no front gate, no footpath; Grandma's door opened straight off the pavement through a huge stone wall. And inside was an old conservatory full of geraniums. It was warm and sweet-smelling, the panels of purple and violet glass mixing with the pinks and reds of the plants, throwing dapples of coloured light onto the black and white mosaic floor.

Sitting in her kitchen we had tea from a huge brown teapot, with plain cake, a loaf of bread and Grandma's home-made quince jam. One of my treasured possessions is a letter from my Grandmother to my Mum when she was first married, containing the recipe for that cake. It was my Dad's favourite. And so was quince jam.

If walls had ears, perhaps they could also tell tales of how these old gardens were created and how the delicious orchard fruits of autumn – apples, pears, plums,

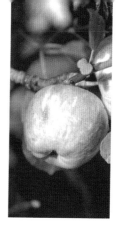

greengages, damsons and quinces – were put to use in the kitchens of old houses. For the fruits of autumn have always been picked and preserved, or stored, for tasty additions to a dull winter diet. Pickles, jams, jellies and chutneys of all kinds can be made with autumn fruits and are a popular way of using windfalls. Fruits can also be bottled or dried for special treats at Christmas and New Year, or used for baking in many ways.

It all seems a far cry from the supermarket where you will probably buy the ingredients for the recipes below. But it is good to know that some of the delicious old varieties of fruit are being saved from slipping into a forgotten era and may be around in greater quantities in future years.

Only you will know if the fruits from the trees in your own garden are good enough to eat, or better for cooking. If you are shopping for fruit, buy Bramley apples if you can and cook flavoursome, firm pears, such as Comice and Williams. The best plums are Victorias. Damsons are delicious fruit to cook with and I use them whenever I can get hold of a good supply. Best of all at this time of year are wild brambles, of course! If you know of a good source, away from a busy roadside, keep it secret and enjoy the treasure trove.

Pears Poached in Green Ginger Wine

INGREDIENTS FOR 4 PEOPLE:

4 dessert pears. These should be roughly of equal size. Select a round-shaped pear, such as Rocha, Williams or Comice. Try to find pears that have a good stem.

500ml water.

500ml green ginger wine.

400g granulated sugar.

2 strips lemon peel.

1 tbsp lemon juice.

Piece of root ginger (about the size of your thumb) peeled and sliced.

A bowl of cold water with a large squeeze of lemon juice added.

METHOD:

Take a medium/large saucepan big enough for the pears to stand in. **Pour** the water into the pan, add the lemon peel and root ginger. **Dissolve** the sugar in the water over a medium heat. **Bring** to the boil and simmer for 15 minutes until syrupy, allowing time for the flavour of the lemon and ginger to develop. **Add** green ginger wine and lemon juice. **Cut** the top off each pear, retaining the peel and the stem. **This** is going to be replaced on each pear as a "lid" in the finished dish. **Place** the tops in the bowl of cold water and lemon juice. (This will prevent the pears from going brown during preparation). **Peel** the pears carefully. **Take** a thin slice off the base of the pear to make it flat so that it can stand in the saucepan. **Place** the pears in the bowl of water and lemon juice while you are preparing each one in turn. **Stand** the peeled pear on a board and, using an apple corer, gently push down through the pear to remove the core.

The object is to have a whole, hollow pear, ready for poaching in the syrup. **Stand** the pears in the hot syrup and simmer for approximately 10 minutes. **The** amount of time will depend on how ripe the pears are. **Do** not overcook. **The** flesh of the pear should be soft and yielding, but still intact. **To** ensure that the pears are covered by the syrup during cooking, place a circle of greaseproof paper over the pears. **This** helps to keep them covered and avoids discolouration. **Before** removing the pears, add the tops and cook for a further 2 minutes at most. **Transfer** the pears and tops to a serving dish. **Pour** over the syrup and leave to cool completely. **Keep** refrigerated before serving. **At** The Three Chimneys, we fill the cavity of the pears with fresh blueberries, blackcurrants or brambles before serving. **We** put the lids on top and serve with a spoonful of the syrup and home-made stem ginger ice cream. **Warm** chocolate sauce is also a delicious accompaniment. **Excess** syrup can be frozen and re-used to poach more pears at a later date.

Plums in Spiced Port Wine

This is a delicious compôte of fruit that can be made, cooled and kept in the refrigerator. Serve chilled with homemade cinnamon ice cream, natural yoghurt or crème fraîche.

INGREDIENTS:

12 dessert plums, preferably Victorias, cut in half and stoned.

250ml ruby port.

125ml water.

2 strips lemon peel.

1 cinnamon stick, broken in half.

4 juniper berries.

4 cloves.

2 cracked cardamom pods (optional).

2 bay leaves.

55g soft dark brown sugar.

METHOD:

Put the port, water, lemon peel, spices etc and sugar into a medium-sized saucepan. **Bring** to the boil slowly, allowing the sugar to dissolve completely. **Stir** from time to time. **Add** the plums. **Bring** back to boiling point and then reduce the heat to a low simmer. **Place** a lid on the saucepan and allow the plums to cook very gently for about 5 minutes. **Remove** from heat and pour into a bowl. **Cool** completely and then refrigerate, preferably overnight, before serving.

Autumn Pudding

Summer Pudding is a well-known recipe, using all the delicious soft fruits available during the summer months. This is my version for the same pudding using autumn fruits. Instead of making it in a pudding basin in the traditional way, we make this for the restaurant in a rectangular dish, which is much easier to serve. You can do it either way at home. If you have been cooking with damsons and have surplus damson juice as a result, use the juice to make extra syrup to serve with the finished pudding.

For 6–8 people you will need a rectangular dish (approx 30cm long x 24cm wide x 5cm deep). **You** will need a 3 pint pudding basin if you are going to make it in the more traditional way.

INGREDIENTS:

At least 1 white medium sliced loaf, of reasonable quality, crusts removed.

350g cooking apples, thin sliced (weighed when peeled and cored).

200g pears, thin sliced (weighed when peeled and cored).

200g plums, cut in half and stoned.

100g brambles, washed and picked over.

Half a lemon.

225g soft light brown sugar.

1 cinnamon stick, broken in half.

METHOD:

Put the sliced apples and pears into a medium-sized saucepan that has a well-fitting lid. **Add** 2 tbsp water and the juice of half a lemon. **Add** sugar and cinnamon stick. **Bring** to boiling point, very slowly, allowing time for the sugar to dissolve and start to create syrup. **Stir** all the ingredients together gently, put the lid on the pan and leave to simmer on a low heat for approximately 10 minutes. **Add** the plums and brambles and cook for a further 5 minutes. **The** fruit should be softened, but still retaining its shape. **Line** the base and the sides of the dish (or pudding basin) with the sliced bread. **Layer** half the cooked fruit with some of the juice over the bread. **Place** a second layer of bread over the fruit. **Add** a second layer of fruit and some more juice. **Finish** with a layer of bread and pour all the remaining juice over the surface of the bread. **The** number of layers of fruit and bread could be increased depending upon the size of your dish. **Cover** with a double sheet of greaseproof paper and place a weight on top. **Leave** overnight in a cool place to allow plenty of time for the juices to develop, soak in and soften the bread. **We** sit a similar-sized dish on top of the pudding with a large bag of sugar to act as a weight on top of the dish. **If** you are using the basin method, place a plate on the top of the bowl and a weight on top of that. **The** whole pudding should be turned out upside down from the pudding basin when it is served. **The** pudding can be cut into neat squares when it is made in a rectangular dish, which you may find easier to serve. **Extra** syrup from cooking damsons or brambles can be used to serve with the finished pudding, poured over the top.

HAWTHORN TREES thick with white May blossom will always remind me of when Steven was born in 1979. Lindsay was my late-September rose in 1981. By the autumn of 1983, as I faced the prospect of being a young mum at home for yet another Croydon winter, I began to take stock of the future.

Steven was due to start school full-time the following Easter. Lindsay was a bright and active toddler. Sarah was another part of the equation. By then, she was a loveable but rebellious punk with jet black hair and spiky earrings, studying for A-levels at 6th form college with good university prospects.

I had been asked to do a few freelance jobs from home while the children were babies. One of these could have provided enough work for me to start a small PR business of my own, but I decided against it. It was still a man's world in business and I had outgrown their striped suits and leery ties. Eddie was

Mark Seymour The Mill House, Fintry, Glasgow G63 0YD
Telephone 036 686 342

Property for Sale

THE THREE CHIMNEYS RESTAURANT
COLBOST
NEAR DUNVEGAN
ISLE OF SKYE

SPECTACULAR LOCHSIDE POSITION WITH UNRESTRICTED VIEWS
EASILY ACCESSIBLE AND SITED ON MAIN TOURIST ROUTE
CLOSE TO POPULAR TOURIST ATTRACTIONS
WELL KNOWN RESTAURANT (55 COVERS)
SELF CONTAINED OWNERS ACCOMMODATION (3 BEDROOMS)
NEWLY BUILT KITCHENS   ½ ACRE GROUNDS
RIGHT OF ACCESS TO LOCH DUNVEGAN
PLANNING CONSENT FOR ONE CHALET
RESTAURANT LICENCE
PRICE £47,500

Mark Seymour M.R.V.M, M.Inst.M
SPECIALIST ESTATE AGENT TO THE LICENSED TRADE
SALES PURCHASES VALUATIONS CONSULTANCY INVENTORIES

growing tired of his long, stressful hours as a driving instructor, coping with the ever-growing problems of city traffic congestion. The time had come to change our lives.

We both wanted to move to Scotland, as we preferred the thought of the children growing up and going to school there. However, we had little idea of what to do for work, as we were both seeking a career change, together with the move.

Our dinner table dreams of running our own bistro began to take shape. It would be simply styled with lots of chunky pottery and candles in bottles. I would be proud to prepare and serve some traditional Scottish dishes, using all the old names: Neep Bree, Cranachan, Mussel Brose, Stew with Mealie Dumplings, Cullen Skink, Shepherd's Pie and Stovies.

As our ideas became more tangible, we began to look randomly for suitable property. My Mum tried to help by sending us the property pages from The Scotsman with possibilities ringed in pen. The Scottish Borders was our first choice as a suitable area near my native town of Peebles. I had dreams of taking over somewhere like the historic Tibbie Shiels Inn by St Mary's Loch, near Selkirk, or the Howgate Inn near Penicuik on the road to Edinburgh. An enormous part of Scotland's recorded culinary heritage is associated with this whole area. Perhaps I had romantic notions of becoming a second Meg Dods, running a modern-day Cleikum Club. Who knows?

Certainly, my personal business plan was based more upon historic fantasy and belief in Scotland's unsung kitchen prowess, than it was on any financial scheme of things. Being recognised as an internationally acclaimed restaurant with awards, stars and accolades was completely beyond our ken, let alone our wildest dreams.

And then it happened! The post had arrived one wet day in February. I had requested a copy of a commercial property company's composite brochure. Flicking through it at the kitchen table with a mug of coffee, I found a picture of The Three Chimneys in Skye. It was for sale and within our price range. This had to be fate!

To cut an even longer story short, we decided to go to Skye and view the property. Off we went, one cold weekend in March 1984. Eddie had never been to Skye before. The weather was dreich – there is definitely no other word for it. We flew to Glasgow and hired a car. We drove north by Glencoe and Fort William to Kyle of Lochalsh, through showers of sleet, under grey skies, by steely lochs and a brown, barren landscape.

We arrived in Portree, the main town on the Isle of Skye, having booked ahead into one of the hotels that happened to be open. I believe we were the only people staying and aroused great curiosity from the elderly receptionist as to "Why is a young couple here on their holidays in March?" The bedroom was freezing

From sheltered gardens
128

cold, heated by a portable oil-fired radiator that no-one had switched on. The bathroom was a long way down the corridor and the window was jammed – open. We were the only guests having dinner that evening, bar one man on his own. (Had an inspector called?) After a meal that reminded me of all the criticism of Scottish food that had annoyed me so much in the past, we took ourselves off to the hotel lounge – and drank alone. It was Saturday night.

"I can't possibly live here!" was Eddie's determined verdict.

The next morning it was snowing, but we drove off towards Dunvegan on the other side of the island. As so often happens, the weather completely changed halfway. We reached the bend in the road at Flashader. From there we could see the distinguished flat tops of the twin hills, Macleod's Tables, bathed in sunshine under a bright blue winter sky.

The Three Chimneys at Colbost, beneath Macleod's Tables, on the single-track road from Dunvegan to Glendale, had been under new ownership for some seven years since my original visit in 1974. The owners had extended the dining area into both of the ground floor rooms of the cottage and built a brand new kitchen at the back of the building. The public toilets were encompassed within this new extension and it was no longer necessary to venture outdoors to the shed in the back-yard!

To my mind, these were all vast improvements upon how I remembered the restaurant in my younger years. The new kitchen, with its commercial-sized cooker, steak grill and big double fryers looked 'the business', even though I had never cooked on anything like this size of equipment in my life.

The privately accessed flat above the restaurant provided perfect accommodation for the children and ourselves, plus Sarah during her holidays. This aspect was crucial to our final decision.

We could do it! We could buy this way-of-life business and move to Skye. We gave no real thought to where our customers were going to come from, a marketing strategy, finance, or long-term business plan. But we could indulge our restaurant fantasy within the cosy stone walls of a crofter's cottage by the sea in beautiful north-west Scotland.

First, we had to sell our house in Croydon. We went home and put it on the market that week. Our new life had begun.

As sure as eggs is eggs

COOKING IS as simple as boiling an egg. That was the reassuring message suggested by the picture of Delia Smith on the cover of her original, best-selling book, *Complete Cookery Course*. Holding a smooth brown egg, plain, but perfect, this famous shot was sure to make everyone feel confident that great meals from little eggs grow.

And how that book sold. I swear it became the household bible of my generation and beyond, because it taught us all how to cook the classical basics, as well as daring new dishes such as Chilli con Carne, Moussaka and Coq au Vin. Now we could take everything in our stride, from rice and pasta, to bread, cakes, puddings and preserves. Sunday lunch or Christmas dinner? No problem!

Nothing fazed us girls who wanted to experiment with cooking seductive dishes. Call cooking the 'new sex'? If so, then I guess we invented that too.

The well-over-forties have been cooking their way into their men's hearts for years. After all, we were not able to dash into the supermarket to buy ready prepared 'cover versions' of those wickedly new dishes. They did not exist in packets. Microwaves were unknown. Takeaways were slightly frowned upon. If we wanted to know about Lasagne al Forno, we had to work out how to make it ourselves. And joy of joys! It was all in Delia.

Delia may have been subjected to criticism from some of today's TV celebrity chefs, but it makes me mad when I read their opinions of her supposed incompetence. Sorry guys, but Delia was there long before you. It was her drive to equip the people of Britain with all the practical skills of cooking that baked the bread you are all buttering now.

Pardon the pun, but some male chefs have an incredible ego. I have a theory that bears this out. Women are expected to cook well domestically from an early age and are derided if they cannot. On the other hand, if a young man shows a special aptitude, high praise is bestowed upon his talent and he is given every encouragement to do well, or become a professional. Although we need to encourage

hundreds more women to join the industry, it is one of the few remaining careers to allow male chauvinism to dominate.

One of the UK's most infamous world-class chefs was once reported as saying that he never employs women, as they are only good for three weeks out of four. I'd like to retort by saying that some men I have worked with are only good if their football team is winning – that day.

Come on girls! The world of professional cooking may be hot and steamy, but if I can succeed, then anyone can. Women *can* stand the heat in the kitchen. We win hands-down for stamina and being able to cope with organising more than one job at a time. Apart from anything else physical, we usually cook because – simply – we love it.

Cooking can be as simple as boiling an egg, but some dishes are more

daunting than others. Soufflés can be temperamental, but they are not impossible. Use the same basic method which follows, but adapt it with different ingredients for a wider variety of ideas for different menus and occasions. Choose your eggs with care. I make use of my local supplies of organic eggs. I know exactly where they come from and trust how the hens are fed.

Now, take four fresh eggs...

Soufflés

For each of the following recipes, which are suitable for 6–8 people, you will need:

1 x 1 litre soufflé dish OR 8 x size 1 ramekins.

A roasting tin, or similar, large enough to stand the dish

or ramekins in.

BEFORE YOU START TO MAKE THE SOUFFLÉS:

Pre-heat the oven to Gas Mark 5 (190°C, 375°F). **Pour** hot water into the roasting tin to a depth of approximately 2cm. **Place** the tin on the top shelf of the oven if you are using ramekins, or on the centre shelf if you are using a large soufflé dish. **The** water should be piping hot by the time you put the soufflés in the oven. **Butter** the soufflé dish or ramekins liberally. **Coat** the base and sides of the dishes with a half-and-half mixture of fine white breadcrumbs and very finely grated Parmesan cheese. **Put** the dishes to chill in the refrigerator before using.

Smoked Ham and Haddie Soufflé

Smoked haddock (undyed, of course) with ham or bacon is a traditional combination of flavours. It works well for breakfast, a light lunch, or high tea. This recipe makes a very popular starter for a dinner party. Your friends will love it and soufflés always make a great talking point.

INGREDIENTS:

225g smoked haddock fillet.

50g finely chopped smoked ham.

300ml milk.

2 sprigs of parsley, including the stalk.

1 bay leaf.

Freshly ground black pepper.

Freshly grated nutmeg.

Finely grated rind of half a large lemon.

1 small onion, finely chopped.

1 tbsp finely chopped parsley, or mixed herbs such as

chervil, lemon balm and dill.

4 large eggs.

40g plain flour.

40g butter.

METHOD:

Put the milk, parsley sprigs, bay leaf, pepper, nutmeg, lemon rind and onion into a wide saucepan. **Bring** gently to simmering point and lay the haddock fillets into the milk. **Cover** with a lid and leave to poach very gently over a low heat. **This** will take 5–10 minutes, depending upon the thickness of the fish. **When** it is ready, the fish will begin to flake apart easily. **Try** not to let the milk overheat and curdle. **Lift** the fish out of the pan and leave aside to cool. **Strain** the milk through a sieve and discard the parsley and bay leaf. **Retain** the onion with the lemon rind. **Pour** the milk into a measuring jug. **You** need 300ml to make the sauce. **Top** up the quantity, if necessary, with a splash of extra milk, or cream. **Remove** any skin or small bones etc from the fish and break it up with a fork. **Tip** the onion into the bowl with the flaked fish. **Add** the chopped ham, plus the extra freshly chopped herbs and mix everything together.

TO MAKE THE SOUFFLÉ:

Melt the butter in a saucepan and stir in the sieved flour to make a roux. **Gradually** stir in the milk which the fish was cooked in, stirring all the time until you have a thick sauce. **Leave** this on a very low heat to cook gently for 10 minutes.

Separate the eggs and beat the yolks into the sauce. **Add** the flaked haddock mixture and chopped ham. **Stir** well. **Check** seasoning. **As** the smoked fish and ham is salty, you may not need any more, just a few twists of freshly ground black pepper. **Last** of all, whisk the egg whites in a clean, greasefree bowl, until they reach the soft-peak stage. **Stir** one spoonful of the whites into the fish mixture to loosen it. **Fold** the remaining egg whites into the fish mixture with a large metal spoon, with a cutting and folding motion. **Put** the mixture into a large soufflé dish, or divide it between the ramekins. **The** mixture should fill the dishes to just below the indent of the rim. **Place** the dishes in the hot water in the roasting tin in the pre-heated oven. **Be** careful, as the water will be hot. **The** large soufflé will take 30–35 minutes to bake in the centre of the oven. **The** smaller ones will take

15–20 minutes on the top shelf. **The** soufflés will rise and look golden brown on the surface. **They** should be slightly crisp on top and soft in the centre. **Some** may rise more evenly than others, but don't worry about it. **Serve** them immediately from the oven, as they sink very quickly.

Alternative Ideas for Soufflés:

Follow the above instructions, but make the sauce with plain milk, instead of milk used to poach the fish. **You** can then add a variety of items to the sauce, after beating the egg yolks into the basic sauce mixture. **Try…**

225g of mixed brown and white crabmeat or 225g chopped smoked salmon, or flaky hot-smoked salmon. (Omit the onion, but add the lemon rind and freshly chopped herbs, plus salt and pepper to taste.)

225g finely grated mature Cheddar cheese. Add the finely chopped onion to the melted butter when you make the roux and allow it to soften before adding the flour, followed by the milk. (Omit the lemon, but add a heaped tablespoonful of freshly chopped parsley and chives, plus salt and pepper to taste.)

In another recipe, I use 175g of a delicious, hard Scottish goats cheese called Bonnet, together with 2 ripe pears, peeled, cored and chopped small, with a teaspoonful of finely chopped fresh rosemary and lemon rind, plus salt and pepper to taste. The onion is not necessary in this recipe.

THE DAY before we were due to exchange contracts on the sale of our house in Croydon in 1984, we received a letter from the Bank of Scotland rejecting our loan application. We needed this to complete our purchase of The Three Chimneys and had been negotiating since April. It was now the beginning of October and we were due to be out of the house by the following midday.

Having been given a firm, verbal go-ahead we had been pressing the local Scottish bank manager for written confirmation for many weeks and had been repeatedly assured that a letter was on its way. The letter we tore open in excited anticipation was curt and to the point. The Bank of Scotland had decided against backing our move to Skye with a business loan of £25,000. We were absolutely devastated. The final piece of the whole jigsaw was missing.

Our date of entry to The Three Chimneys was planned to coincide with the date the local licensing court sat in Portree. It was customary in those days to exchange contracts and take over as licensee at the same time. We had two weeks to raise the money.

We left Croydon as planned, to spend the interim two weeks with my parents in Peebles, before making the final leg of our journey to Skye. Our Inverness lawyer introduced us to the manager of the Royal Bank of Scotland in Kyle of Lochalsh. We arranged a meeting and Eddie and I headed north-west on the appointed day.

On the way, I made one of the worst overtaking manoeuvres of my driving career and misjudged how near I was to the next bend in the road. Consequently, I hit it too fast and spun the car, clipped the crash barrier and narrowly missed an oncoming bus. Thankfully, no-one was hurt, just badly shaken. I remember it was one of the last occasions I wore a skirt and high heels. When I got out of the car, my legs were like jelly. The lady whose car I had been overtaking wound down her window and offered me a valium! We drove slowly to the Bridge of Orchy Hotel, where we stopped to check the car, drink coffee and telephone the Royal Bank to explain our delay.

We finally arrived in Kyle, several hours late. Nevertheless, we seemed to create a good impression. Our determination to make a success of a new life in Skye was, by now, stronger than ever. Since our first spontaneous visit, our ideas had taken on a more definite form with the semblance of a real business plan. We secured our loan. It was much less than we wanted, but it was enough – just – and besides, we were no longer in a position to negotiate.

We completed our journey to Skye on Tuesday 16th October 1984. The car was packed to capacity, with more under polythene on the roof rack. The children sat on their duvets and pillows in the back seat. Our first night was spent in the Benlee B&B in Portree, overlooking the harbour. The owners, Mr and Mrs MacPherson, were so welcoming, making a point of offering us a dram after supper as we sat and chatted in their lounge.

On Wednesday 17th October, Eddie attended the licensing court with our lawyer. Having secured the licence for our new premises, we were in a position to complete the purchase.

Together with the children, we met the previous owners in the Caledonian Café in Portree's Wentworth Street, where we signed and exchanged the various documents.

The Three Chimneys was ours. We drove over to Colbost in sunshine mixed with heavy showers. I was soon to learn that this kind of weather always creates beautiful rainbows in Skye. That day was no exception and we drove under several bright arcs along the winding road.

Moving home is an unnerving experience for everyone. Relocating your whole life in a completely different world can shatter self-confidence. We had sold almost all of our personal items of furniture. Our beds were the largest items we moved with us. With a struggle, we just managed to squeeze our double bed up the tiny staircase. The bedrooms were cold and felt damp despite my efforts to make everything homely on our first night. There was no central heating. Two obsolete gas wall heaters of the type used in caravans were the only heating in the ground floor rooms. One of our early discoveries was that these created

horrendous condensation, literally making the cold interior stone walls run with water.

The restaurant kitchen was also my new family kitchen. I despaired many times trying to handle the large equipment. The first batch of ten loaves I ever baked was instantly dropped on the floor. The heat from the thin, flat metal trays seared through my domestic oven gloves, burning the tips of all my fingers. I wept as I asked myself why I had ever imagined I could be a chef. Knives were another early challenge. The only ones I had were a set with red handles that Eddie and Sarah had bought for me as a present from Habitat a few years before. Buying good knives and stout oven gloves was an early priority.

A restaurant critic recently wrote in a newspaper article about us that: "only a romantic with nerves of steel would ever have dreamt of opening a restaurant here..." True, I had plenty of romantic ideals, but from the day we moved in, I experienced many, many nerve-breaking moments. And still do, to this day.

On October 17ᵗʰ
Eddie and
Shirley Spear
moved in to the

THREE CHIMNEY'S RESTAURANT
COLBOST
NR. DUNVEGAN
ISLE OF SKYE.

(Telephone: Glendale 258)

Opening April 1985
Skye's the limit!

Roast nuts, friendship and real fires

BLEAK NOVEMBER days are brightened by all the preparations for the festive season. One of the early signs that Christmas is coming are red string bags full of shiny brown nuts on the supermarket shelves. I have eaten hot chestnuts roasted over an open fire only once in my life. There is a first time for everything and the occasion was a memorable one.

A dear friend had been home for Christmas to her cottage in Skye. A crowd of us had gathered around her fire, red wine in hand, full of fun, chat and laughter. She produced a gift she had received from her husband that year. It was an antique chestnut roaster; rather like a cross between a pair of small bellows and one of those round toasted sandwich makers that sits directly over the gas cooker flames.

"Obviously for the girl who has everything!" she laughed, as she put the chestnuts between the two halves of the roaster, clipped it together and placed it on top of the hot coals in the open fireplace.

To me, this was real Christmas!

The roasted chestnuts were hot and soothing in my hands. The skins had split and when peeled, the warm nuts had an unbelievable velvety texture, sweet and savoury, all in one delicious mouthful. They were not hard and crunchy, but soft and yielding with an undeniable comfort factor. I knew then why I'd seen

numerous scenes in old films over the years, of people huddled around the street brazier on freezing, foggy nights; warming their hands with hot nuts, while warming their hearts and chilled spirits with conversation and friendship.

The chestnuts we eat are not the same as the big shiny conkers we used to string and knot for gang fights. They are not the hard, green spiky fruits we kicked amongst the autumn leaves to find, in a serious bid to be the playground 'conqueror'. The horse chestnut tree with its giant, hand-like, five-finger leaves is quite different from the sweet, or Spanish chestnut tree that provides the nuts we eat. The chestnuts for sale in the shops at this time of year mostly come from the south of France, or Italy. British summers are not hot

enough to ripen the sweet chestnut, but despite this, they have been a winter delicacy in this country for generations. Chestnut stuffing for the turkey or goose has become a popular ingredient of our traditional Christmas dinner, for example.

The fruit of the sweet chestnut tree looks more like a small round hedgehog with its green spiny husk. Like its spiked conker cousin, the green husks split when ripe and the brown nuts are the shiny treasure to be found inside.

The Romans are said to have introduced the sweet chestnut tree to Great Britain. Apparently they made a kind of porridge with the dried nuts ground and mixed with milk. Cockney friends in commuter-belt Croydon, shocked at our news that we were moving to faraway Skye, exclaimed in horror that: "Skye is so far north, the Romans are still looking for it."

Perhaps the Romans never tried Scottish porridge, but they are said to be responsible for introducing the pheasant to our shores. This also was a great move, because pheasant and chestnuts make a perfect combination. Great tasting dishes are made with the addition of all the winter vegetables, fruits, dried fruits and herbs we know and love in cooking at this time of year. Celery, shallots, parsnips, apples, prunes, raisins, sage and thyme, can be added to soups, pâtés and pot-roasts. Chocolate and chestnuts is another delicious combination for a Christmas dessert such as Chocolate Chestnut Log.

Cooking and peeling raw chestnuts is time-consuming. Rinse the chestnuts and slit each one with a sharp knife and place them in a large pan. Cover with water, bring to the boil and simmer for 15 minutes. Remove the pan from the heat, but do not drain. Remove the chestnuts from the water one at a time and peel the skins. The cooked and peeled chestnuts can be used in any of the following recipes. However, I have used cooked and peeled whole chestnuts, now widely available vacuum-packed and preservative free, in tins and packets. This speeds up the whole cooking process and makes it much easier for the cook – particularly at Christmas!

But if you get an opportunity, try roasting some chestnuts over hot coals with good friends. There's nothing quite like it.

Celery, Apple and Chestnut Soup

INGREDIENTS:

2 heads celery.

2 large onions.

2 large cooking apples.

2 x 240g tins whole chestnuts.

50g butter.

1 litre vegetable stock.

Half a litre full cream milk.

Double cream to serve.

Freshly ground sea salt and black pepper.

2 tsp freshly chopped thyme.

1 tsp lemon juice.

METHOD:

Separate the celery sticks and wash them thoroughly. **Discard** any that are particularly coarse and trim the rest. **Chop** the celery, including the leaves, quite small. **Peel** and chop the onions about the same size. **Peel**, core and chop the apples. **Place** them in a bowl, cover with some fresh water and the lemon juice until ready to use. **Melt** the butter in a good-sized soup pot. **Stir** the celery and onion in the hot melted butter, put the lid on and leave on a very low heat for 5–10 minutes until the vegetables have softened and are turning pulpy. **Add** the apples. (The water and lemon juice can go in too.) **Stir** well, season with salt and pepper and add the fresh thyme. **Pour** in the hot vegetable stock. **Bring** the soup to the boil, then cover and simmer over a low heat for at least 30 minutes. **Add** the chopped chestnuts and simmer for a further 10 minutes. **Add** the milk and liquidise the soup. **It** can be left chunky, or can be completely smooth. **Check** seasoning. **Stir** in some double cream before serving.

N.B. This soup could be made with turkey stock at Christmas and some of your leftover cooked turkey could be chopped and stirred into the soup with the chestnuts.

Game Terrine of Pheasant with Raisins and Chestnuts

This may look ambitious, but with patience, it is easy to do. A home-made game terrine in the fridge is a great standby for Christmas entertaining. It can be made several days in advance and kept chilled before slicing and serving as a starter, or a light lunch dish. I serve it cold with Mulled Cider and Apple Sauce and include the recipe below.

If you do not have an ovenproof terrine dish, a loaf tin will do fine. I use a long thin one that measures 26cm long x 10cm wide x 7cm deep. An ordinary 2lb loaf tin is also suitable.

INGREDIENTS:

2 fresh oven-ready pheasants.

350g minced belly pork.

150g unsmoked streaky bacon, chopped very small.

(Altogether, you will need 2 x 250g packs of streaky bacon. Once you have taken this quantity from one pack, the rest will be used to line the container, as described below.)

120g large seedless raisins.

1 tbsp Armagnac.

120g chopped chestnuts.

1 heaped tbsp fresh parsley, sage and thyme, mixed and finely chopped.

Finely grated rind of half an orange.

2 tsp grainy mustard.

Freshly grated nutmeg.

Freshly ground sea salt and black pepper.

TO MAKE THE TERRINE:

Choose your container and brush the inside lightly with olive oil. **Set** aside 150g of bacon for the meat mixture and use the rest to line the container. **Flatten** and stretch each rasher on a board with a palette knife. **This** makes them longer and suitable for lining the terrine, while leaving a surplus overlapping the sides of the container, to fold back across the meat once it is packed inside. **Pour** the Armagnac over the raisins and leave them aside to soak it up. **Remove** the whole breasts from both pheasants. **Keep** the two that look the best for the centre of the terrine and chop the other two very small. **Put** the chopped breast meat in a mixing bowl. **Remove** as much of the remaining meat from each of the pheasants as possible. **Chop** it very small and add it to the bowl. **Add** the minced belly pork and the chopped streaky bacon. **You** should have approximately 750g of meat in total. **Add** the mustard, the orange rind, the herbs, some grated nutmeg and seasoning. **Mix** it all together well. **Your** fingers will be best for this job – clean of course! **Roughly** chop the raisins that have been soaking in Armagnac and add them to the meat mixture together with the chopped chestnuts. **Mix** again. **Take** a little less than half the quantity of meat mixture and pack it firmly into the bottom of the tin, which should be lined with streaky bacon and ready to use. **Again**, clean fingers are best for this job. **Lay** the two whole pheasant breasts down the centre of the tin on top of the first layer of meat. **Keep** them central, away from the edges of the container. **Now** pack the remaining meat mixture tightly on top of and all around the pheasant breasts. **There** will be enough meat mixture to fill the container to the top. **Bring** the surplus bacon overlapping the sides of the container back across the top of the meat mixture. **The** terrine mixture will now be completely encased with bacon in the container. **Cover** the terrine with a layer of greaseproof paper and then a layer of foil to seal it. **Place** the container in a deep roasting tin, half-filled with hot water. **Carefully** lift this on to the centre shelf of a moderately hot oven (Gas Mark 5, 190°C, 375°F). **Bake** the terrine for 1 hour. **Carefully** remove the terrine from the oven and peel back the foil lid. **Check** that the juices are clear and that the meat feels firm to touch. **If** necessary, return the terrine to the oven for a further 15 minutes. **Once** cooked, leave covered and place a heavy weight on top of the terrine. **Leave** it to cool completely, with the weight on top. **Turn** out the terrine carefully from the container. (**The** pheasant mixture should still be completely encased in the bacon). **Wrap** the finished terrine in fresh paper and foil and chill in the refrigerator before slicing and serving.

Mulled Cider and Apple Sauce

Warm 250ml cider in a saucepan together with 4 cloves, 1 broken cinnamon stick, a sprig of thyme and a shaving of orange rind. **Leave** this to infuse in a warm place.

Meanwhile, peel, core and chop 2 large cooking apples. **Place** in a saucepan with a dash of water, the finely grated rind of half an orange and 2 teaspoonfuls of caster sugar. **Cover** the saucepan with a lid and cook over a low heat until the apple is soft and pulpy. **Stir** in 250g of soft light brown sugar and liquidise the apple to make a purée. **Add** the strained cider, stir well and sieve through a fine mesh to make the finished sauce. **Can** be served hot or cold.

Pot-Roasted Pheasant with Cider, Apple and Chestnut Cream Sauce

INGREDIENTS FOR FOUR PEOPLE:

2 oven-ready pheasants.

2 medium onions, chopped small.

2 sticks celery, chopped in small chunks.

2 cooking apples, peeled, cored and chopped in small chunks.

12 whole shallots, peeled.

240g tin whole chestnuts.

250ml dry cider.

125ml double cream.

Freshly ground sea salt and black pepper.

2 sprigs each of fresh thyme, sage and parsley.

2 shavings orange peel.

25g butter plus 2 tbsp olive oil.

METHOD:

Wash the pheasants, inside and out, and pat dry. **Season** with salt and pepper. **Make** a small bundle of herbs for each pheasant and place it inside the cavity of the bird together with the orange peel. **Heat** the oil and butter in a heavy-based frying pan and brown the birds all over. **Set** them aside. **Soften** the chopped onions and whole shallots in the same pan, add the celery and apple and stir together well. **Season** lightly. **Pour** the cider over the vegetables and heat through. **Pour** this mixture into a deep, ovenproof dish. **Sit** the pheasants on top of the bed of vegetables. **Spread** a knob of butter over each bird. **Cover** with greaseproof paper and foil to make a 'lid'. **Put** the dish in the centre of a moderately hot oven (Gas Mark 6, 200°C, 400°F) and cook for 1 hour.

TO SERVE:

Remove the cooked pheasants from the dish and keep warm. **Pour** the remaining contents of the dish into a wide saucepan. **Add** the whole chestnuts. **Bring** this sauce mixture to the boil and then simmer slowly, with the lid off, to allow the sauce to reduce and thicken slightly. **Just** before serving, add the cream. **Check** seasoning and stir in 2 teaspoonfuls of freshly chopped thyme. **Heat** through again. **The** finished sauce should be thick and chunky. **Place** a spoonful of sauce on each plate. **Carve** the breast meat and place it on top of the sauce. **Check** the leg meat for tenderness and serve it too, if you wish. **I** serve this dish with parsnip mash and baby sprouts with crispy bacon. **A** slice of caramelised Cox's apple makes a perfect garnish.

TWO WEEKS in sunny Cyprus is like finding heaven on earth in November. When we closed the restaurant doors, we abandoned all thoughts of business with a huge sigh of relief and flew off to our favourite island in the sun.

In the early years, we took the children with us. This became too disruptive to their schooling as they grew older and we began to steal holidays on our own. More recently, our commitment to running the business all year round has made holidays more difficult to obtain.

Returning to Scotland about one month before Christmas always hit us with a few shockwaves. Everywhere would be brightly lit and sparkling in preparation for the festivities of the coming weeks. The shops would be overflowing with gifts, cards and decorations. Had another year flown past already?

My Christmas list always included shopping for the more mundane essentials to take home with me to Skye. A trip to the bookshops was also a priority. By now, most of the new restaurant guides would be on the shelves. I dreaded opening their covers and finding my way to Colbost through the wafer-thin pages. I have often likened the experience to opening the horrid brown envelope that contains your school examination results.

With a silently pounding heart and a dull ache in the pit of my stomach, I would read our critiques with mixed emotions. No entry was ever perfect, or accurate, or quite fair. But there it

would be in print for all the world to see. And there was absolutely nothing I could do about it. Having committed every minute of every day for many months, providing the very best I could within the constraints of our location and complete lack of professional help, I would be left feeling totally crushed and demoralised by even the tiniest criticism. I had to try harder. Every chef must have these feelings, but perhaps, being female, I have to admit to being more sensitive.

I gave up writing protesting letters to the editors of food guides many years ago. Instead, I began to concentrate on dealing with inspectors direct during the many 'de-briefings' I endured, mostly late at night. It is never going to be pleasant to be told that your food is not good enough to match this or that grading. Every minute detail is considered, from the serving temperature of the soup, to *the texture of the pastry in the dessert. Did the vanilla ice cream have enough vanilla flavour? Was the mashed potato mashed enough? Did the rosemary in the lamb gravy overpower all the other flavours of the dish? I would argue my case. The average restaurant-goer would be shocked to know how seriously each inspection is taken.*

I was reduced to tears by one inspector as I sat opposite him, listening to him telling me his mother made better apple crumble. Seeing my state of near-breakdown, he leaned across and patted me on the knee.

"There, there," he said. "Have you had a hard day?"

Another inspector left me so deflated, I packed my bags and left home, driving off into the night, howling with tears of anger, mixed with despair and exhaustion. I vowed that night to give up altogether. I never

wanted to cook another meal again in my life. A few years later, the same inspector told me he had only ever tasted food as fresh and true to itself at Gordon Ramsay's London restaurant. Naturally, I was flattered, albeit a little amused.

For many years, the thing I have resented most of all is being compared with every restaurant across the UK. I have never wanted to be a London restaurant in the wilds of north-west Skye. I have never wanted to be a classical French restaurant. From the very start, I wanted to make my own mark and have my own style; to be proud of Scottish things and to serve Skye's fresh, local produce in the best way I knew how. We became the round peg in the guide books' square hole. The fact that our house style did not fit every inspector's criteria has never made our food less special in the eyes of our customers.

However, I was determined not to change our style purely to gain specific guidebook status. The guide inspectors would have to accept us and reward us for all that we represented in the culinary world. The AA was the first major organisation to agree to my way of thinking. Making the most of fresh local produce in the simplest ways, allowing the natural flavours of the food to triumph in their own way, were among the reasons why we were eventually awarded the coveted 3 AA Rosettes.

It soon became apparent that our customers loved everything we represented. We began winning awards in Scotland in 1989. In 1990 we won the Macallan/Decanter Scottish Restaurant of the Year. For the ceremony, we were flown by helicopter from Skye to beautiful Kinnaird in the heart of Perthshire in its late-autumn glory. The flight was spectacular. Mentally, I began

Guest lists, friendship and real fires

152

writing my book during the course of our journey home. We flew into the sunset over Morar and Eigg. As we drifted with the clouds over the Cuillin Ridge towards Colbost, the whole of the Duirinish Peninsula seemed to have been spread out before us like a giant table-setting. The panoramic view from the helicopter displayed every detail. From The Minch on the left to Loch Dunvegan on the right, everything was distinguishable and could be seen in its perfect place, right out to Dunvegan Head.

We have won many awards in Scotland since 1990, including major Taste of Scotland awards. Compared with the food guides, the best aspect of these is that they are all customer-led. The customer votes for the winner, based upon their own experience of each establishment.

In March 2002 we were informed that we had been placed at No 28 on Restaurant magazine's list of the World's Top 50 restaurants. We were stunned by the news, but delighted to be there as the only Scottish restaurant and one of only five in the UK. At first it seemed too huge an accolade to live up to. But upon

further investigation I came to realise that our location and ambience, our style and unpushy service, had been considered as being as important as our fresh local food.

I was thrilled! At last we had been given recognition as a real restaurant. We could easily live up to this new status by being true to ourselves and to everything we had ever worked towards. Just for once, I felt proud of all we had achieved.

Wrap up th

eftovers

LEFTOVERS. What did we do before clingfilm was invented? How did we cope before the days of cavernous fridges and deep freezers?

Vivid Christmas memories are usually childhood ones. One of mine is of my Mum covering the cold turkey carcass with grease-proof paper and, for want of anywhere more suitable, putting it back inside the oven for overnight storage. The scullery, with its stone floor and lino, was always chilly enough.

I will never forget her anguish the following day. She discovered that a mouse had climbed into the back of the oven via the gas pipe and had celebrated its own private Christmas Dinner, foraging its way all over the meaty bones. I can remember my own feelings of

dismay when all the lovely leftovers were well and truly dumped in the dustbin. There was no turkey soup and sandwiches that year; no cold stuffing to go with the leftover bread sauce and cold roasties.

I shall respectfully defer to all superior curry makers and decline to suggest that anyone should try my recipe for turkey leftovers. Instead, I'll suggest a way of using some leftover mincemeat of the fruity kind.

When did you last serve Baked Stuffed Apples? Rather than making yet more mince pies, resurrect this old-fashioned favourite. Stuffed with mincemeat, particularly if it

is home-made and laced with lots of brandy, baked apples make a real family pudding. Spoon the syrup over the top and serve them with Proper Custard.

Other kinds of leftovers are usually the result of over-indulgent shopping. What is it about Christmas that makes everything on the shelves so irresistible? As well as all the traditional, seasonal goodies, we are now bamboozled with a choice of fruit and vegetables from every corner of the world. Really, we do not want to eat strawberries in December, but we simply cannot resist them.

Some exotic fruits are more seasonal than others. These are flown in from foreign lands, sun-kissed, secretly special and just a wee bit sinful. If you are like me, you will feel compelled to buy the juicy ripe ones, like fresh pineapple, one of my favourite foods.

My early memories of pineapple and fruit salad exist in the era of

'that' turkey. In those days, pineapple rings and fruit salad came out of tins, syrup-laden and soft textured. A big family, we always argued over whose turn it was to have the cherry. Mum spooned the diced fruit into the pudding plates and we solemnly passed them round the table, having been suitably admonished.

This was also the era of Mum's first dinner parties. The menu was so impressive. Home-made potato croquettes, mixed frozen peas and tinned sweetcorn kernels and a whole roast gammon joint studded with cloves, pineapple rings and glacé cherries. I thought it all looked amazing, but had to go to bed before the guests arrived.

About this time, I also first set eyes upon a real pineapple. I remember there was an exclusive fruit shop somewhere near the West End of Princes Street. I cannot remember the name, but the vision of the shop window is very clear in my mind; a high, plate-glass window,

curved and bevelled at each corner, framed on either side by moulded round poles with a ball at top and bottom. The window display always intrigued me, because there was hardly anything to it; perhaps a basket or two with a few choice pieces of fruit in each.

One Christmas, a solitary pineapple sat centre stage. It was all alone at window-sill level, in pride of place. What on earth was it?

I was amazed at Mum's explanation. She was aghast at the price. I could not get the exotic image out of my mind. And later I asked her if I could have it for Christmas.

For your family Christmas, try a refreshing Exotic Fruit Salad, using all those delicious and luxurious fruits that may have been gracing the fruit bowl on your sideboard for several days. They will be longing for the opportunity to be eaten! The recipe for Fresh Pineapple in Caramel Syrup can be served on its own, but it can also form the base of the Exotic Fruit Salad which follows. I serve this with home-made coconut ice cream, or lime and ginger sorbet, but a good quality vanilla ice would do. The

Cardamom Crisps are a perfect accompaniment too.

Fresh halibut is my all-time favourite white fish and cooking it with fresh Skye oysters and champagne seems a suitable celebratory way in which to serve it for a special Christmas meal with a difference. As we serve champagne by the glass in the restaurant, we occasionally have some leftover in the bottle. Using it for the Velouté Sauce is better than letting it go flat and to waste! The oysters, of course, are fresher than fresh from Loch Harport.

Baked Stuffed Apples

INGREDIENTS:

4 large cooking apples, preferably Bramleys.

25g butter.

Approximately 250g Christmas mincemeat.

4 level tbsp soft light brown sugar.

150ml cream sherry.

METHOD:

Pre-heat the oven (Gas Mark 4, 180°C, 350°F). **Wash** the apples. **Carefully** remove all of the cores from the apples using an apple corer. **Score** the skin around the fat middle of each apple and slice a small piece off the base so that the apple can stand steadily in the baking dish. **Use** a small, sharp-pointed knife for this. **Stand** the apples in a shallow ovenproof baking dish. **Fill** each of the apple core cavities with the mincemeat. **The** quantity will depend upon the size of the apple. **Put** a knob of butter on each apple and sprinkle thickly with brown sugar. **Pour** the sherry all around the apples. **Put** the baking dish on the top shelf of the oven and bake for 1 hour. **Spoon** the shiny syrup over the top and serve either hot or cold with cream or Proper Custard.

Proper Custard

Follow the recipe for Drambuie Custard on Page 31 but omit the Drambuie.

Fresh Pineapple in Caramel Syrup

Take 1 large fresh pineapple. **Remove** the skin and slice it into rings. **Remove** the centre core from each slice. **Place** the pineapple slices into a shallow serving dish, overlapping in layers. **Take** a piece of root ginger about the size of the top of your thumb and slice it very thinly. **Pour** 250g of caster sugar into a wide, heavy-based pan. **Melt** it slowly over a low heat until it becomes liquid and golden. **Pour** 500ml of white wine over the caramelised sugar. **Add** the root ginger. **Simmer** until the liquid is reduced by one third. **Strain** this syrup over the pineapple slices and leave to cool. **Serve** chilled with the syrup poured over the pineapple, with fresh cream or ice cream and Cardamom Crisps.

Exotic Fruit Salad

You can make this with any combination of exotic fruits of your own choice. **I** like to use the Pineapple in Caramel Syrup as a base and add an assortment of other fruit as available. **For** the salad in the photograph, I used **mango, fig, kiwi, clementine, banana** and the juicy seeds from a **passionfruit**. **Arrange** the fruit on the plate in a similar way to the illustration, or mix all the ingredients into a bowl and serve in the more traditional style. **You** can be as flamboyant and festive as you like with this recipe. **It** is a great way to 'wrap up' the leftovers!

Citrus-Baked Halibut Fillet with Oyster and Champagne Velouté

My advice for cooking this dish is to prepare the sauce first of all and then prepare the fish ready to go into the oven. As fresh white fish will spoil if it is not served immediately, time the cooking of the fish to coincide with the serving time. The sauce can be prepared in advance and reheated before serving. The oysters should be added at the very last minute.

STAGE 1: PREPARE THE HALIBUT.

INGREDIENTS FOR 4 PEOPLE:

4 x 175g pieces of halibut fillet.

25g unsalted butter.

Half a lemon.

Freshly ground sea salt and white pepper.

A few lemon balm leaves, or sprigs of chervil, or fennel, or all of these.

2 sprigs of flat parsley.

1 bay leaf.

METHOD:

Butter a suitable ovenproof dish. **Scatter** 2 slices of lemon, the lemon balm leaves and/or additional herbs, sprigs of parsley and bay leaf, into the dish. **Season** lightly with sea salt and white pepper. **Place** the fish in the dish, in a single layer and spaced apart. (If you are not cooking the fish immediately, prepare to this stage, cover the dish with clingfilm and refrigerate it before finishing the dish as follows.) **Season** the fish lightly with salt and pepper. **Squeeze** a few drops of lemon juice from the remaining piece of lemon onto each piece of fish. **Carefully** cover the whole dish with a sheet of foil. **Try** to avoid the foil touching the fish. **Make** sure the dish is sealed completely around the edges. **Place** the dish in the centre of a pre-heated oven (Gas Mark 5, 190°C, 375°F). **Bake** for 10–15 minutes, depending on the thickness of the fillet.

STAGE 2: PREPARE THE OYSTER AND CHAMPAGNE VELOUTÉ.

INGREDIENTS:

12 fresh oysters in the shell.

900ml good quality fish stock.

350ml champagne (or dry white wine as an alternative).

100ml dry vermouth.

6 shallots, finely chopped.

50g closed cup mushrooms, washed and finely chopped.

25g unsalted butter.

500ml fresh double cream.

METHOD:

Open the oysters and carefully remove the oyster in one piece. **Put** the oysters in a bowl with the juice from the shells. **Keep** refrigerated. **Melt** the butter in a wide saucepan with a heavy base. **Cook** the chopped shallots in the hot butter, until soft but not colouring. **Add** the chopped mushrooms and stir together with the shallots until soft. **Pour** the champagne and dry

vermouth over the shallots and mushrooms. **Retain** a high heat and reduce liquid until it has almost disappeared and has a syrup-like consistency.

Pour in the fish stock, bring back to the boil and retain a high heat until the liquid has reduced by half. **Add** the cream, bring back to the boil and maintain a rolling boil for approximately 5 minutes until the liquid is beginning to get thicker and coats the back of a wooden spoon. **Strain** the sauce through a fine sieve and set aside until ready to use. **Before** serving, reheat the sauce. **Immediately** before serving, add the oysters to the hot sauce, together with approximately 8 tsp of the oyster juice. (N.B. more juice will be released from the oysters too.) **Bring** the sauce back to near-boiling point and remove from the heat for serving. **The** oysters will only take a few seconds to poach in the hot sauce until they just hold their shape. **If** they are allowed to cook for too long, they will quickly become rubbery. **Taste** the

sauce before serving. **The** oyster juice is naturally salty. **It** should be unnecessary to add any seasoning, but you may wish to adjust the finished sauce with a little more cream. **The** texture of the finished sauce should be smooth, velvety and of easy pouring consistency.

TO SERVE:

Remove the cooked halibut from the oven and place on hot serving plates. **Carefully** lift the poached oysters from the sauce with a slotted spoon and place them around each piece of fish. **To** ensure that any tiny particles of oyster shell are removed, strain the remaining sauce through a fine sieve into a warm jug and pour it around the fish, coating each of the oysters as you pour. **Serve** with fresh vegetables of your choice.

Cardamom Crisps

INGREDIENTS:

125g butter.

175g caster sugar.

1 egg, beaten.

50g desiccated coconut.

175g self-raising flour.

Finely grated rind of 1 lemon.

The seeds of 2 cardamom pods, crushed.

INGREDIENTS:

Cream the butter and sugar until light and fluffy. **Add** the egg and beat thoroughly. **Add** the coconut, the flour, lemon rind and crushed cardamom seeds and mix thoroughly until mixture forms a firm paste. **Form** into small balls about the size of a £1 coin and place each one, well spaced apart, on a greased baking tray. **Flatten** each ball gently with a palette knife before putting the baking tray into a pre-heated oven (Gas Mark 5, 190°C, 375°F). **Bake** for 10–15 minutes until biscuits are golden brown. **When** you remove the baking tray from the oven, flatten each biscuit for a second time until quite thin. **Remove** from the tray and cool on a wire rack. **Store** in an airtight tin until ready to use. **Dredge** with icing sugar before serving.

AS I HAD the most plates, and the largest saucepans, it became customary for me to cook the family Christmas dinner. When we were closed in the winter months, it was a perfect family time to celebrate the holiday and spend some time together.

I have always loved the magic of Christmas. I love decorating the tree, wrapping surprise gifts, writing cards to distant friends. When we moved to Skye, we were determined to spend our first Christmas and New Year on the island in our new home. It was a frugal Christmas and full of uncertainty. By this time, we had begun to encounter some of the minor 'downsides' of life in Skye and The Three Chimneys in Colbost.

We had made new friends, but not firm friendships. I missed my supportive circle of young mums in Croydon. Lindsay, for all of her 3 years, missed the company of the children she had met and played with through a variety of toddler groups and activities. Steven quickly settled into his new school environment and seemed to thrive with his new routine. I cooked and baked and planned ahead. I read and researched recipes, planning ingredients, finding suppliers. I was full of anxiety and sapped of self-confidence. Eddie, meanwhile, was ecstatically painting, mending and building, loving being outdoors in the crisp winter sunshine.

We took time out to explore the far-flung corners of the island, seeing some beautiful wild sights in the depths of winter. I must have spent hours simply gazing out of our front windows across the loch. The view never stayed the same for more than a few minutes. I literally could watch the weather 'happen' as it rolled in from the Atlantic, across The Minch and into Loch Dunvegan. The rocks could be lashed by high seas and white spume on one day; the next it could be so calm, the absolute peace and stillness was disturbed only by the sound of a seagull's wings taking off over the water.

I was completely spellbound by my new surroundings; the ever-changing views, the mountain peaks in all weather, sunsets over the Hebrides silhouetted on the horizon, the moonlit nights and dark skies heavy with star clusters. These things will never change.

In other ways, Skye was a very different place when we first arrived. The Free Church still held a

domineering influence over everyday life. In those days, I definitely would not have hung out my washing to dry on a Sunday. There were no shops open, nor petrol or newspapers for sale. Many people were strict about not working or travelling on the Sabbath and many more went to Church regularly. The sale of alcohol was strictly licensed.

Christmas was hardly celebrated in public. New Year was the major holiday. That first year, I was quite astonished to discover how little the local shops stocked up and prepared for Christmas. It was difficult to find even a Christmas card for sale. No fuss was evident.

There will always be conflicting opinions of the role the Church has played in Skye and how the incoming population made waves of change.

The everyday way of things is more relaxed nowadays, but some believe this to be to the detriment of island life. The sanctity of Sunday was always very special and I am glad that I had the opportunity to cherish it for a few years.

By the time this book is published, almost exactly eighteen years since we arrived in Skye, the supermarkets in Portree will be open seven days. Instead of taking delivery of the Sunday papers on the following Monday afternoon, we may be able to buy them after midnight at the all-night petrol station.

Now we have a Christmas tree in Portree's village square and coloured lights strung across Wentworth Street. Trees and lights now twinkle in the front windows of many island houses, lighting up the long, dark,

mid-winter nights. And The Three Chimneys is now open almost all year round. Christmas dinner is served in The Restaurant and Bucks Fizz is poured at breakfast for guests staying over the holiday in The House Over-By.

Changed days from those early years when the extended family gathered round the Christmas dinner table in paper hats, pulling crackers, cracking jokes. I cannot deny that I miss those occasions, but our lives have all moved on.

Will life go full-circle? Will the family cook for me one day, while I tell tales of the time when Granny was the chef at a famous restaurant in the Isle of Skye?

Time will tell...

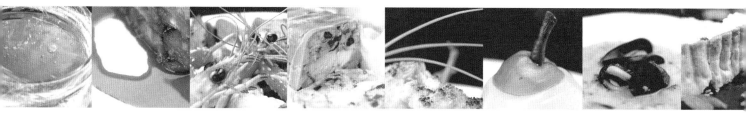

INDEX

Thank you

Of all the unexpected things to happen during this hectic year of 2002, the latest is a nomination for a Scottish Thistle Award in the Individual Excellence category. The annual Thistle Awards made by VisitScotland, recognise excellence in the Scottish tourism industry. I am enormously proud to be on the shorlist, but have to protest that there is no such thing as 'individual excellence' in this World. I could never have achieved success on any scale without the support and skills of all those around me – our staff, good friends and close family. Eddie and I are a partnership through and through.

Our staff at The Three Chimneys win praise from our guests and customers at all times and I certainly could not run our 5-star Restaurant with Rooms without any of them. The office and housekeeping staff are as crucial to our whole operation as the restaurant and kitchen brigades. As our story goes back eighteen years, those who have worked at The Three

Chimneys in the past are just as important to me as those who are here now. There are too many to name individually, but I hope that some of the events and occasions described in the book will bring back memories for everyone, of the part they played in the whole story.

Special mention must go to Diana Mackie, landscape artist and designer extraordinaire, for her commitment to our success, her incredible talent and above all, her constant support, encouragement through the toughest times, and true friendship.

Without Alan Donaldson's stunning photographs, there would be no book. I will let his work speak for itself, but want to add what a privilege it has been for me to work closely with him on all the food shots. He too, has been enormously supportive of our business development here in Skye and keeps me up to date with all the city chefs' gossip. A few shots appear in the book taken by John Paul of

Inverness, who was responsible for our original, excellent brochure photography. I have also used a few of the beautiful shots taken by Eric Thorburn and first featured in Homes and Interiors Scotland Magazine, in 2001.

I can honestly say that my life has never been the same since I met our marketing adviser and graphic designer, Peter McDermott. Since he helped to relaunch The Three Chimneys with its brand new corporate identity and created our now-famous logo, we have worked together on many projects, including our brochure. However, this book is the ultimate testimony to his talents as a designer. Quite literally, the whole project took shape under his direction and determination to make me have faith in its success. What a friend he has been to Eddie and I.

Nan, Sarah, Steven, Lindsay and Eddie – thanks for just being yourselves and staying beside me.